T0054464

Animal Magic

Animal Magic

A Handbook of
MYSTICAL ENERGIES
AND ENCHANTMENT

RIEKA MOONSONG

wellfleet
press

Dedication

This book is dedicated to my children, Hailey and Jake. You both are the light in my darkness, and I am thankful every day that I get to be your mom. I love you both so much.

First published in 2023 by Wellfleet Press, an imprint of The Quarto Group, 142 West 36th Street, 4th Floor, New York, NY 10018, USA T (212) 779-4972 F (212) 779-6058 www.Quarto.com

Wellfleet Press titles are also available at discount for retail, wholesale, promotional, and bulk purchase. For details, contact the Special Sales Manager by email at specialsales@quarto.com or by mail at The Quarto Group, Attn: Special Sales Manager, 100 Cummings Center Suite 265D, Beverly, MA 01915 USA.

10 9 8 7 6 5 4 3 2 1

ISBN: 978-1-57715-395-5

Library of Congress Cataloging-in-Publication Data

Names: Moonsong, Rieka, author.
Title: Animal magic : a handbook of mystical energies and enchantment / Rieka Moonsong.
Description: New York, NY, USA : Wellfleet Press, 2023. | Series: Mystical handbook ; 18 | Includes bibliographical references and index. | Summary: "In Animal Magic, unlock the magical powers, guidance, and protections offered by animals while calling on mystical animal energy with magic, spells, and meditations to strengthen your craft"-- Provided by publisher.
Identifiers: LCCN 2023020915 (print) | LCCN 2023020916 (ebook) | ISBN 9781577153955 (hardcover) | ISBN 9780760385562 (ebook)
Subjects: LCSH: Animal magnetism. | Magic. | Psychic energy (Psychoanalysis) | Incantations. | Human-animal communication.
Classification: LCC BF1156.O2 M66 2023 (print) | LCC BF1156.O2 (ebook) | DDC 154.7/2--dc23/eng/20230530
LC record available at https://lccn.loc.gov/2023020915
LC ebook record available at https://lccn.loc.gov/2023020916

Publisher: Rage Kindelsperger
Creative Director: Laura Drew
Editorial Director: Erin Canning
Managing Editor: Cara Donaldson
Editor: Amy Lyons
Cover Design: Beth Middleworth
Interior Design: Rebecca Pagel

Printed in China

Contents

Prologue

$\sim\!\!\bullet\!\!\sim$

Take a walk with me into the woods . . . Through the forest canopy, the bright sunbeams reach the earth. There is great energy and magic to be found within this place. You listen closely, not just with your ears, but with your heart and soul as well. You know that the animals here have messages to deliver and magic to share. The birds are singing to you, their melody soft and sweet. The squirrels chatter as they roam the branches in search of pine nuts for their winter stash. The journey along the earthen path opens into a great meadow where wildflowers dance and the bees gather for their pollen. A great stag steps out of the trees. His antlers are majestic, a conduit for messages from the world of Spirit and a connection to the Divine. He dips his head in acknowledgment of you and as he does, that message comes through, giving you the answers you were seeking. You thank him before you part ways . . .

Introduction

Hello there. Welcome and merry meet. If this book has found its way to you, there may be animals wishing to share their magic with you and that are now working on your behalf. Perhaps you have been curious about what kind of magic the animal kingdom can bring into your life. If you already work with the energy of animals, then maybe you're looking to dive deeper.

As a born witch, I have always felt the magical energies of animals. I spoke to them as a child and frequently saw animal guide spirits as well. I worked with them instinctually, allowing those animals to assist and guide me. Through my magical and shamanic training, I now have a deeper understanding of what it truly means to have animal guides and a familiar.

A magical teacher once asked me to figure out the process in which I connect with these guides; how do I know which one to call upon in various situations? What I learned was that there was no process for me. It is something that is instinctual and because of my deep connection to them, they show up for me when I need them without having to call upon them. It is my hope that through this book, you too will learn the beautiful significance they have in our lives, as well as how to easily connect with the animals so that they may assist you in your magical practice and how to be open to the messages they are bringing to you.

Within these pages, you will learn about some of the history pertaining to animal magic. You will learn invocations to call various animal guides to you so that you can begin to work with them and their energies. You will gain knowledge regarding the different energies of animal messengers and guides, how and why they come into your life, and how to incorporate their power into your rituals and spell work. You will also leave with a deeper understanding of what it means to connect with the animals and how to work with them in your magical practice. There are spells and workings included here that are designed to help you on your journey with animal magic.

At the end of the book, you will find a reference section with the magical tools mentioned throughout the book to help you better understand them and be able to work with them in relation to animal magic. For those who are new to witchcraft and working with magic, note that invocations and spells are two different things; an invocation only calls the energy to you, while a spell incorporates that energy into your magical working.

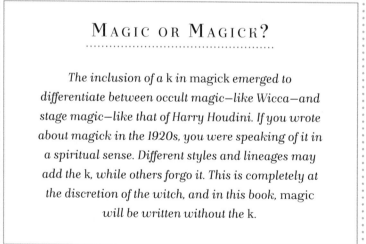

MAGIC OR MAGICK?

The inclusion of a k in magick *emerged to differentiate between occult* magic—*like Wicca—and stage* magic—*like that of Harry Houdini. If you wrote about* magick *in the 1920s, you were speaking of it in a spiritual sense. Different styles and lineages may add the* k, *while others forgo it. This is completely at the discretion of the witch, and in this book,* magic *will be written without the* k.

An Origin Story

To find out where we are going, we must first start at the beginning. As with most things that have become part of our culture, or in this case, magical and spiritual practices, there is an origin story. How and why something came about is often just as important as the actual practice itself. When we know the why, the other stuff seems to fall into place easier.

WHAT IS ANIMAL MAGIC?

Animal magic can best be described as being able to access the energy and power of an animal for magical and spiritual workings, but it does go deeper than that. It is calling upon those energies to assist with our witchcraft in general or very specific spells and rituals. It is being open to receiving messages and guidance from the animal kingdom. Animal magic is making connections to and forming bonds with animals that inhabit the physical plane as well as those that roam the metaphysical realms and beyond. It is understanding them in a more personal way so that we can better understand ourselves, the natural world around us, and our own magic.

Many believe that animal magic has been with us for as long as we have known how to tap into the energies of the natural world and the Universe. Animals are just another aspect of nature. Much like the plants that hold their own metaphysical properties, so too do the animals.

Across the globe, you will find stories, myths, legends, and folklore that include animals. The ancient peoples linked animals to their deities, the celestial bodies, and naturally occurring events, such as storms and other weather patterns.

In ancient Egypt, Mesopotamia, Greece, and Rome, we see evidence that there were magical practitioners. Effigies of animals or their bones have been found to be a part of these practices. These workings ranged from protection and defensive magic to outright curses. Animals were also involved in healing and divination as well as the way into the afterlife. Animals were known

messengers and held power and favor with the gods. They came as omens, both good and evil.

In the Mesoamerican region, a nagual is a person who could shape-shift into their animal counterpart. The belief that this person could tap into the power and insight of their animal by having a deep spiritual connection with it is called nagualism.

In small Ukrainian villages, they rely heavily on livestock for their prosperity, so some of their animal magic comes in the

form of protection for their own private stock as well as blessing the animal husbandry to ensure fertility for future generations. Rituals and incantations were performed for reproductive magic for the animals as well as for the milk that would be generated in the postpartum period.

Animals and animal symbolism are also seen throughout the occult beliefs of medieval Europe. They were part of various practices, such as healing, protection, and love spells, and even used to poison and kill. As Christianity began to rise, we saw the decline in the belief that animal magic served as a benevolent force. It was not discounted, but instead became tied to witches and was made into something evil. Any animal deemed to be a witch's familiar was killed alongside the person accused of witchcraft.

WITCHES, SHAMANS, AND WISE PEOPLE

We are the workers of magic, those who can reach into the void and bring forth energy to create and manifest. We feel the world of Spirit and can communicate with the entities that inhabit it. It should come as no surprise that those who have these abilities can also feel the energy of the animals and are capable of hearing their messages. We have been called many things—witches, shamans, and wise people—and while there are actual distinctions between them, we all know that there is a world of "other."

It was once widely accepted that animals had their own power and magic. Somewhere along the way, this was lost. Throughout much of Europe, including Scotland, Germany, Ireland, and France, those who did maintain some of the old ways, including the knowledge of animal helpers, were persecuted as witches. Some continued to work with animal energy in secret, finding ways that would not draw suspicion.

In other places in the world, the wise people and shamans of the tribe or community were allowed to freely continue to work with animals and their magic. Much of the information we have on the energy of animals today is because these people passed down this knowledge.

The Q'ero people in Peru are the last living descendants of the Incas, having fled to the mountains to survive the Spanish conquest in the 1500s. Through oral tradition, their beliefs and traditions were kept alive. The shamans of these people are called Paqos. The Paqos came to believe that their knowledge was meant to be shared with others because it is crucial to preserving life on Mother Earth. They have animal totems that reside in each of the four directions—north, east, south, and west—and they believe all animals are sacred and have something to teach us.

⚘ ANIMAL MAGIC LORE ⚘

The amount of folklore surrounding animal magic is staggering when you look at how widespread it is. Cultures from all over the world include animals in their myths and legends. Many cultures have animals taking part in their creation stories. There are tales of animals and the gods, those of good and evil, and even superstitions. In the lore of the Q'ero people, it is said that when the great eagle of the north and the great condor of the south fly together once again, the Earth will awaken, as will her guardians. It will be a time when our consciousness soars and we return to more natural ways. The eagle will lead us with his great vision, and the condor with his open heart.

Shape-shifting is a common thread when it comes to animal magic in folklore. You see this theme in many cultures. Sometimes it is the animal that seeks to become human, and other times it is the human that transforms into an animal. For example, the selkies in Scottish lore are seal creatures that become human to marry and then return to the sea. There are also instances where the gods, witches, or sorcerers intervene, causing the transformation.

In Chinese and Japanese folklore, we see animals linked to their zodiac systems. These animals cycle over a twelve-year period based on the orbit of Jupiter, the planet of luck, fortune, and prosperity. It is believed by these cultures that the animal designated to one's birth year has influence over the personality of that person.

Serpent magic is also widespread through many cultures and appears in myths and folklore because of its ties to the cycle of life, death, and rebirth. This is seen in the symbol of the ouroboros, the circular snake eating its own tail, also known as a symbol of eternity. However, the snake is also shown to be evil, such as the serpents upon the head of Medusa and in the biblical myth of Eve and the serpent in the Garden of Eden.

Animals have been given value in cultures as being harbingers of either good or bad fortune. Ravens are often said to foretell death. This is not surprising, as they are the symbol of the Morrigan, the Celtic goddess of battle and death. Owls are symbolic of wisdom because of their ties to the Greek goddess of wisdom, Athena. Rabbits herald the return of spring and are called upon for fertility magic.

Animals have a place in the world's stories, which show how revered they are for their energy and their magic.

⊷⊛ THE ANIMAL REALM ⊛⊷

Discussing the animal realm can get a bit complicated because there is not just one place where we can find animal energies. We have animals here in the earthly plane that interact with us. They can lend their power and magic as well as deliver messages and offer guidance. The realm of Spirit is also a place where animals reside. This can include our pets that have passed and who choose to stay in this realm instead of fully crossing the Rainbow Bridge. They might choose to stay for various reasons, one of those being that they feel we still need them. The realm of Spirit is also one of the places where an animal familiar may come from before they choose their incarnation in the earthly plane. Animal spirits can move freely from one realm to another, including the astral plane and the etheric.

Unlike the world of the fae, there are no designated portals that animals need to use to cross between realms. Most animal guides and messengers that come in spirit form can traverse the realms without any trouble. It is actually their intended subject that acts as a beacon for them. Witches, shamans, and other magical people can be considered portals to realms where animal guides and messengers originate. It is our magic that draws them to us, thereby creating a space for them to come through easily and efficiently so they can deliver messages and offer us guidance.

In some of the shamanic traditions, there is a separate world where animal guides and totems reside. There are three worlds total: the Middle World is what we live in and is our current reality. The Upper World is the one of ascended masters. These are beings who would arrive there because of their spiritual attributes, such as Gandhi, Buddha, Jesus, spirit beings from other realms, and even angels. The Lower World is the one that belongs to the animals. This is where we go to meet our animal guides and messengers.

Getting to the Lower World requires a shamanic journey. The guided instruction on this can be found on page 104. There is an entrance into this realm that acts as a portal. This is there for our benefit, so that we may travel there to visit with the animals. This portal can look different to each of us but is almost always something natural. It can be the mouth of a cave, a door that appears at the base of a tree trunk, or sinkholes. There is a guardian at the portal entrance that you will first need to seek permission from to enter the Lower World. The guardian

appears different to each of us. You can also ask the guardian for assistance; remember to thank them.

Knowing the history of animal magic helps us understand why cultures across the world venerate the creatures we share the Earth with. When we can grasp this, it gives us the tools to move forward and begin to understand their energy and the magic they can bring to us.

Understanding Animal Energy

As we have learned, ancient peoples were keenly aware of the mystical and magical properties that each animal held within them. When we started creating "society" instead of tribal communities, we began to lose touch with this knowledge and wisdom. We became arrogant and close-minded in our way of thinking. We separated ourselves from the animals and their magic, wisdom, and medicine. The animals, however, did not forget the bonds that had been forged with magical and spiritual people. This is why they still seek us out today. Those of us who walk the path as witches, shamans, light workers, and healers are in tune with higher vibrational patterns, the realm of "other," and the magic of Mother Earth. We are able to connect with animal spirits and guides in ways that others cannot. Animals come to us to assist us on our journey through life. They lend magic, guidance, wisdom, and medicine to those who are willing to listen, learn, and share this knowledge.

Animals are drawn to us for various reasons. Witches and other magical people have strong connections to the natural elements. Those who practice nature or "green" magic often have frequent wild encounters with animals because animals are drawn

to that person's energy. Animals are often messengers of Spirit, your guides, or the Universe. They come to us to deliver these messages. Animals can also act as a mirror to the emotions or needs that we have regarding a situation. The animal that shows up for us in that moment is validating what we already know and guiding us to a solution. Other times, they show up in our lives so that we may learn from them, to assist us with healing or to help us on our magical path. Make no mistake, the right animal will show up for you when you need it.

✿ ANIMALS AND THE GODS ✿

I f a witch or magical person is one who works with deity, then a particular animal coming to them could be a representation of a god or goddess. Most of the various pantheons, such as Greek, Roman, Norse, Hindu, and Egyptian, have animals that are associated with their deities. Some deities actually transform into those animals. This is called *zoomorphism*. An example of this is the goddess Bast in Egypt morphing into her full cat form. Her usual form is that of a woman's body with the head of a cat. She is the patroness of all cats and their protector. The goddess Isis is associated with birds of prey, scorpions, and cows. A hawk, snake, beetle, or lion holds the energy of the sun god Ra for the Egyptian people.

In the Norse pantheon, Odin is known for his two ravens and wolves. Odin often transforms into a raven to deliver messages. Freya has her fierce battle cats and Thor has two mighty goats that pull his chariot.

The Greek goddess Artemis is the goddess of the hunt, the wild, and the wilderness, and therefore is associated with all wild animals, and the deer in particular. Hekate, queen of the witches, has an owl companion as well as her hounds. The eagle and the bull are representations of the mighty Zeus. And for the Romans, doves are symbolic of the goddess Venus. The wolf is sacred to the war god Mars.

The animals that are tied to specific deities are associated with them because the energy of the animal aligns with that of the deity. While various animal energies can overlap, there are often several distinct characteristics or magical properties that are unique to an individual animal.

⚘ ANIMALS AND THE SABBATS ⚘

J ust like deity associations, specific animals also correspond to pagan Sabbats because of their energies. For example, Ostara, or the vernal equinox, is the celebration of the first day of spring. The rabbit is one of the traditional animals corresponding to this Sabbat. Ostara holds the energy of new beginnings and fertility. Likewise, the rabbit is one of the most common animals linked to fertility magic.

Black cats and ravens have been associated with witches for millennia, so it shouldn't be a surprise that they are animals that correspond to the high holy day of Samhain. This Sabbat is what appears as Halloween on the calendar. Both black cats and ravens hold powerful magic and are known shape-shifters in the magical community. They are also associated with death, furthering their alliance with the day when the veil between the realm of Spirit and that of the living is at its thinnest.

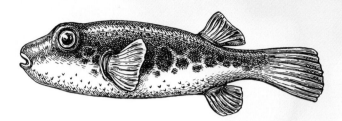

ANIMAL ENERGIES FOR A MAGICAL BOOST

While each type of animal holds its own unique magic, some groups tend to cover a broad energy. Birds, for example, are known to be messengers of Spirit. This is due to the fact that they soar into the heavens and then back down to Earth again. Snakes and other reptiles are known for their powerful transformational energy and magic. They remind us of the importance of letting go of what is no longer serving us, like the shedding of their own skin, so that they may continue to grow. Large mammals, such as elephants, bears, and bison, hold earth energy that is very calming and grounding. Because the element of water is tied to emotions, fish and other water-dwelling creatures often bring messages surrounding our emotions, our emotional well-being, or how different situations are impacting these emotions.

Much like groups of animals that cover a broad spectrum of energy, there can also be different animals that are linked to a very specific energy. This includes those that hold solar and lunar energies. Animals that represent the sun are the lion, bee, ram, eagle, hawk, rooster, and salamander. When someone wants to work with sun energy, one of these animals might show up to assist. The opposite energy of the moon can be found in the wolf, bat, owl, moth, domestic cat, and most big cats, to name a few. These animals can facilitate help when working with lunar magic.

While all animals have something to offer and can help us in our magical practices and workings, there are some that rise above the others when it comes to witchcraft. Animals naturally bring the wilder side of our own nature to the surface, facilitating a deeper connection to the power that lies within us and the natural world.

Some of these animals have been tied to witchcraft for ages, such as the bat, raven, owl, and cat, and others are probably ones that most wouldn't consider very witchy. Calling upon the energy of these particular animals can lend power to spells and rituals, aid in divination, and even facilitate healing. Nocturnal animals have the special gift of being able to assist with shadow work, while a lot of the animals that are out and about during the day can help with vitality as well as happiness and joy. Included with each of the following animals is an invocation that can be said to call upon their energy when it is needed.

BAT

The nocturnal bat aligns with lunar energy as well as that of the earth because a lot of them roost in caves, which are known to be "the belly of Mother Earth." Bats teach about the hidden mysteries and help with deep shadow work while also keeping one grounded and centered. Their echolocation can facilitate journey work that helps one "find their way in the dark." This could be about the magical/spiritual path or the life path in general. The bat is also extremely helpful for spells having to do with communication and can be particularly useful during Mercury retrograde.

INVOCATION OF THE BAT

Journey from the womb of Mother Earth
Echoes in the night to find your way
Never lost within the dark
Seeing what is hidden
With communication and intuition
Dancing in the moonbeams
Heralding change, transition, and rebirth.

BEAR

Similar to the bat, the bear also holds the energy of the night and earth. The two constellations Ursa Major and Ursa Minor represent bears in the night sky, thus holding energies of the heavens and the stars. The bear is also tied to the goddess Artemis. Her name comes from the root word *artos*, which means "bear." Their large size gives them the powerful, grounding energy of the earth as well as great strength. Calling upon the bear, a witch will have access to vast amounts of earth energy but will also be able to stay grounded while working. Bears are also known for their healing abilities because of their earth magic. The bear will happily assist in spells or rituals for protection.

INVOCATION OF THE BEAR

Fierce protector
Bringing strength and courage
Mother bear
Her mighty paws upon the earth
And the cycles of nature written in her fur
Finding balance
Healing.

BEE

Some of the bee's magic comes from their ability to create honeycomb. The honeycomb is a practice in sacred geometry. The honey that is made is a sacred food of the gods. The process of making honey from pollen is that of transmutation, so bees are helpful when it comes to the alchemy of life and when great change is needed. They hold solar energy and are wonderful allies when working with sun magic. Bees are known for their industrious nature. If one needs assistance with motivation, calling upon them is beneficial. They can also assist if one needs help with interactions in groups or working together. They can help achieve harmonious energy within a workplace, family, and a coven. Bees also remind us that one can remain docile at heart but it is sometimes necessary to sting for the sake of protection. They can assist with protection magic.

INVOCATION OF THE BEE

Sweetness of life is found
In service and hard work
To the hive and to his queen
Hundreds of miles on his tiny wings
Life to the flowers and plants he brings.

BUTTERFLY

It's surprising that such an innocuous animal as the butterfly would be associated with witchcraft. Above all else, the butterfly is seen as a symbol of transformation and transmutation. They can assist those in need of it as well. Because of their gentleness, they also help these transitions to come with gentleness and ease. The Greek word for butterfly is *psyche*, so they are often associated with the soul. They will be of value for soul work that includes delving into past lives. Butterflies also facilitate communication with the spirit realm. Because of their bright and often bold coloring, the butterfly reminds us that life should also be bright and can help if one needs assistance in situations where boldness is required.

INVOCATION OF THE BUTTERFLY

Wings unfolding
Transformation complete
"Change is beautiful," she says
Emerging from the chrysalis
Butterfly flitters and dances
Bright and so alive
Oh, the colors of life!
Awakened to the world of soul.

CAT

The cat is revered in many cultures and religions across the globe. They are known for their powerful magic and are one of the most common familiars. During the witch hunts, cats were also persecuted because it was believed that witches could shape-shift into cats and wreak havoc at night. Cats are associated with moon energy, thus making them an ally for spells or rituals that require lunar magic. Many cultures, such as the ancient Egyptians and the Indigenous peoples of Central and South Americas, had cat deities. Even though cats began their alliance with humans more than ten thousand years ago, they still retain their wild energy. Cats can act as a battery for the witch when doing spell work. Because cats have their own brand of powerful magic, they can easily let it flow to a witch.

INVOCATION OF THE CAT

Feline friend
Mischievous and clever
Full of power and magic
Ties to the goddess and the moon
Who stalks and plays
Never forsaking their wilder ways.

The horse has been an ally of humankind for approximately six thousand years, yet they still maintain a wild and untamed energy. They have an even longer history of magical and mythical ties. Like the bat and the bear, the horse also has dual energy, that of the sun and the moon/water. Horses pull the chariot of the god Apollo across the sky, representing the sun's journey throughout the day. Poseidon, the god of the sea, has a chariot pulled by the *hippoi athanatoi*, which are horses with fish tails. Because of the horse's solar and lunar magic, they are particularly powerful during eclipses. Calling upon them for eclipse workings will not only lend a great deal of magic, but also help one navigate it without any issues. Horses are also known for aiding us in travel, so they can assist with journey work as well as astral travel.

INVOCATION OF THE HORSE

Wild spirit, free and untamed
Passion for life
Racing across the open plains
The inner strength
A driving force
Through obstacles
Horse always finds a way.

OWL

The word *Strix* is a genus of owls and is also another word for witch. Owls are creatures of the moon. Their large eyes take everything in, allowing them to see in the dark of night. They are also one of the only animals that can swivel their head to see behind them. Because of these physical attributes, owls lend powerful magic for divination and have the gift of prophecy. They are also known for their wisdom, so don't be afraid to call upon their guidance when it comes to magic. Many believe the owl to be a creature that has been given the gift of being able to travel between the world of the living and that of the dead. Because of this, the owl can help with contacting spirits and ancestors.

INVOCATION OF THE OWL

Silent wings within the night
For owl's wisdom guides
And vision shows
To be still and quiet
And one will KNOW.

RAVEN

Like the cat, ravens have been tied to witches for centuries. Their ebony wings link them to the night and to magic. They are known to be messengers and bringers of powerful magic to those who call upon them. Trust their guidance for spell work and rituals. The raven is associated with The Morrigan, the Celtic goddess of death and battle, so they too are often linked to death. Much like the owl, ravens can assist in communication with the departed. Raven can offer assistance if one feels like they are facing a battle within their own lives. It may come as a surprise to some that the raven is known for intelligence. If you have a problem or puzzle to work out, calling upon them could be of great assistance.

INVOCATION OF THE RAVEN

On ebony wings you soar
Bringing magic in your wake
Raven, keeper of secrets
And deliverer of messages
Fly with me into the unknown
Into the darkness
To bring forth the light.

SNAKE

The snake is another creature that is greatly feared and yet they have so much to teach us. Snakes shed their skin in order to continue their growth and also to rejuvenate. Snakes continue to grow throughout their lives, reminding us that we need to continue to seek growth for our souls. The snake can help one with letting go of what is no longer serving them. Snakes are associated with kundalini energy that rises from the root chakra. They can help clear and balance the chakras as well as facilitate great transformation. The tongue of the snake is constantly taking in information and they pick up on the tiniest vibrations through their scales. Part of their magic is to assist a witch or magical person with collecting information to see how they need to proceed. They will also help one feel out and interpret subtle energetic vibrations. These creatures are masters of hiding in plain sight, so call upon the magic of the snake to assist with cloaking spells. Snakes are also magnificent allies when it comes to helping one establish and maintain healthy boundaries.

INVOCATION OF THE SNAKE

The vibrations of the Earth
Reside within her scales
Whether on the ground
Or high up in the trees
She's hiding in plain sight
One must look deeply,
To truly see without fear,
By shedding what has died,
Its transformation inside
Lovely snake,
Show us how.

⚜ SPIDER ⚜

Spiders are often feared and even have their own named fear: arachnophobia. However, for something so small, they hold a tremendous amount of magic, and making friends with them is in the interest of the witch. Spiders are tied to the Fates, or the Norns; the term "the web of fate" should come to mind. They can help reveal one's destiny. They hold divine feminine energy as well as the spark of creativity. Think about their beautifully constructed webs. Because of this, they are masters of manifestation. Use the magic of the spider's web when assistance with "catching" an idea, a job, or money is needed. Call upon the spider to help with patience. Because most spiders spend a significant amount of time in the shadows, they are beneficial when it comes to shadow work.

INVOCATION OF THE SPIDER

Within the web of life she waits
Spinning threads of destiny
Patience is a virtue
Feminine energy
The creative spark one needs
Or in the darkness
As spider makes her way
The shadows of one's soul on display.

TOAD/FROG

These amphibians have been associated with witches for ages and are known familiars. Like the butterfly, the adult version is very different from that of the juvenile. They make their way from tadpole to adult, and because of this they hold powerful magic for transformation and transmutation. These animals are linked to both earth and water energy and can help one stay grounded while dealing with heavy or intense emotions. Croaking is their way of communicating and they will help one find their own voice. Because these creatures cannot tolerate toxic environments, they are only too happy to remind us that we should not live in toxicity either. They will facilitate letting go of toxic relationships and situations, as well helping us see our own toxic coping mechanisms and behavior patterns so we can move past them. Frogs and toads are nocturnal animals and have deep ties to lunar energy and moon magic.

INVOCATION OF THE TOAD/FROG

Moonbeams shine upon the water's edge
As a harmonious song begins
Ribbits and croaks to help one find their voice
Nestled within the mud,
A creature of earth and water
Bringing balance and grounding
While emotions surface and swirl
Finding attunement to one's environment
For frog and toad cannot survive
Where toxic energy lies
Letting go of what no longer serves
The transformation begins.

✦ WOLF ✦

The wolf is tied to lunar energy and is also known as a shape-shifter. Consider all the stories about werewolves. Most witches follow the moon phases and time spells and rituals accordingly. A wolf is a powerful ally for lunar workings. Wolves are also the epitome of wild energy. While some may hesitate to call upon this wilder energy, sometimes it is necessary. The wolf can also be called upon to help one follow their instincts. A wolf may also come with its pack, lending even more power. It can aid in workings for familial ties or other relationships as well as being able to work effectively in a group. If you work in a coven, wolf is an animal that might serve well.

INVOCATION OF THE WOLF

Paws fall silently upon the earth
Instincts a driving force
A howl calls out into the night
The family gathers 'round
The time to hunt draws near
Standing in their power
Wolf, leader of the pack.

✿ WHEN THE ANIMALS COME TO US ✿

Animals come to us for many different reasons, in different forms, and in different ways depending on what is needed for each individual person. Animals may come to us in a corporeal (physical) form or in spirit form. They can also come to us in our dreams. Perhaps someone is new to magic and has not yet opened up to hearing the messages that the animals bring in spirit form. That animal messenger or guide is more likely to show up in a physical form to deliver the information it has to give. Sometimes a physical form is also more startling, so a person will take notice as opposed to dismissing the same animal in a dream. If a person sees a snake on a hiking trail, they will remember that experience but they may easily forget that it came to them in a dream a couple of weeks ago.

These animals come to us as messengers, guides, familiars, and power animals and to deliver animal medicine. What are the differences between these and how do we recognize them?

BEING OPEN TO
ANIMAL MESSENGERS

An animal messenger is an animal that comes to a person to specifically deliver a message from their higher self, the Universe, Spirit, their guides, their ancestors, or a deity. These messengers can come in corporeal form, such as seeing a deer on your hike or an owl in the tree in your backyard. Animal messengers can also come in spirit form in a dream. They are merely a visitor sent to you with a message. They may be there for a minute or even a few days, depending on the complexity of the message or how long it takes you to acknowledge it.

When animals come to us to deliver messages, it can be easy to dismiss them. It's just a hawk sitting in the tree, right? How can one learn to listen to these messages? Simply put, be open. Don't discount the things that are coming through. Society conditions us that it is "crazy" to listen to those voices that come through and even crazier to trust and follow them. If you see a hawk and suddenly know the answer to a question you have been asking, that is the hawk delivering the message to you. Let them do what they came to do, and that is to assist you.

To start out, keep a journal of messages, impressions, and images. Note the date and time and then if there is any later outcome to each one. For example, there is a large raven outside

 as you are leaving your home and its loud CAW! startles you. Suddenly, you know that you should not take a certain road to work that day so you choose a different route. You later learn that there was an accident that happened just as you would have been passing through. This message could have been a simple warning about traffic that would have made you late, or something

greater that saved you from being in the wrong place at the wrong
time and getting into an accident. The more you document, the
more you will figure out what messages are coming through from
animals and how they are relating to your life. For some, this is a
vital step because it is confirmation that what is happening isn't
something that is just in their head.

Messages that animals are delivering aren't always warnings.
Sometimes it has to do with spell or ritual timing. There could
be messages that are from an ancestor or another guide that
you have yet to make contact with. Animals may also deliver
messages from other entities, such as the fae, land wights (land
spirits), or elementals. They can also deliver messages from
departed loved ones.

If you are having issues hearing the messages or finding
it difficult to receive them in general, try this simple spell to
facilitate openness. The crown chakra is at the top of the head.
This is our connection to the Universe, Spirit, and our higher
self. When it is open and freely flowing, we receive messages
more easily.

Spell to Open Crown Chakra to Facilitate Receiving Messages

Use this spell when assistance is needed to receive messages.

You Will Need:

- A purple candle (the color purple aligns with the crown chakra)
- A carrier oil of your choice to dress the candle
- Dried mugwort and clary sage
- Lighter
- A timer (it is acceptable to set a timer on your phone)
- Notebook or journal

Spell Working:

1. Go into your sacred space.
2. As part of the working, you must first dress your candle by rubbing it with the carrier oil of your choice and then rolling it in the dried herbs.
3. Place the candle on your altar.
4. Cast a circle.
5. Light the candle and intone the following three times:

    Messages coming to me
    Help me so that I can see
    Help me so that I can hear
    Help me so that I am open to it.
    (after the third time)
    As I will, so mote it be.

6. Set a timer for nine minutes.
7. Soften your gaze or, if you feel comfortable, close your eyes and clear your mind.
8. When the timer is done, write down any messages that may have come through in your notebook or journal.
9. Let the candle burn out completely.
10. Open the circle.

ANIMAL GUIDES

An animal guide is an animal that comes into one's life as a teacher, to offer guidance, support, protection, power, and wisdom and to deliver messages. They have a personal relationship with the individual.

Like messengers, animal guides can also be in corporeal form or reside only in the astral or spirit realm. Animal guides stay for long periods of time, sometimes for one's entire life. Animal guides are often referred to as "spirit animals" or "totems" in some cultures. They will simply be called "animal guides" here out of respect for other cultures and to avoid cultural appropriation.

How do you recognize an animal guide? An animal guide is often an animal that you feel deeply connected to; sometimes it is your favorite animal. Do you feel a special bond with horses or have you always loved wolves? Do butterflies constantly land on you? Do you often dream of a particular animal? If you notice these things about an animal, wild or domestic, chances are that they are a guide for you.

Another way to confirm whether a particular animal is your guide is to keep track of how and when they show up in your life. If an image of an owl pops into your head every time you are preparing to do spell work or a ritual, then they are likely your animal guide.

If you are still having trouble determining whether you have an animal guide or who they are, try this spell to call them to you.

WORKING TO CALL
YOUR ANIMAL GUIDE TO YOU

Do this ritual to establish if you have an animal guide by calling them to you.

You Will Need:
- A white candle

- Lighter

Spell Working:
1. Place the candle on your altar or in a personal sacred space.

2. Cast a circle.

3. Light the candle.

4. When ready, chant the following three times:

> *Animal guide*
> *If you're truly mine*
> *Make yourself known*
> *So our bond can grow.*

5. Continue to watch the flame of the candle.

6. Take note if you see an animal in your mind's eye. This could also come as a sound such as a wolf howl, a whale song, or a bird call.

7. If nothing showed up for you during this working, let the candle burn for another ten minutes, then snuff it out. To continue the working, relight and burn the candle for the next two nights (a total of three nights). Use the chant each time. (Note: Use caution when working with candles, ensuring they are completely out each time.)

8. Open the circle.

Pay attention to your dreams over the next few nights to see whether an animal makes an appearance. If any of the candle remains, leave it on your altar until you are certain of the working's outcome, then dispose of it.

Once you have established who your animal guide is, notice the messages coming through that are guiding you, such as spell work or a particular herb to use. They will also guide you on your path. If you meet an individual that seems like a spiritual person but you suddenly hear your wolf's howl, that is probably a warning sign that they are not part of your path. Every spell we work, every ritual we perform, and all the intentions that we are setting are part of our path. If you are getting messages about how to go about these, then take note, as this is your guide helping you to align with that path and your purpose here.

✦— FAMILIARS —✦

A familiar is a spiritual being or entity that makes a pact with a witch to assist in their magical workings and lend support, power, and companionship. They can assume many forms, but animals are the most common.

Some dictionaries still have a negative connotation as the definition of a familiar spirit. This shows that while some things are progressing where witches are concerned, long-held beliefs can be hard to break. While familiars are spirits or entities, they are not evil, nor are they demons, especially in the biblical sense. That is a completely different energy altogether.

If you are one of the fortunate who has a true familiar, you know that it is a bond like no other. It goes beyond that of a cherished pet and beyond the connection that one has with an animal guide. Not all beloved pets are familiars. While familiars are also guides, it is important to remember that not all guides are familiars.

Familiars choose the individual that they work with and they can also choose their form. Witches report having a dog, rat, snake or other reptile, or even a bird as a familiar. It is common to have a familiar spirit that will come back to you in another form—reincarnation, so to speak. While the familiar spirit does not die when its animal form passes over the Rainbow Bridge, it is released and may choose to return to you.

Having a familiar is a true gift. They sit in circle with us, lend us their power for ritual and spell work, serve as protectors and guardians, can act as an anchor in this realm when we travel in the astral world, and so much more. They do all of this and still can take on the role of guide and messenger as well as cuddle with us in the evening.

So how can you recognize your familiar? How can you be certain that the adorable pet you love so much is a powerful supernatural being? Again, it is a bond like no other. If you have other pets, take a moment to connect with their energies and feel that bond. If you have an animal guide, reach out and feel that connection, its power, and how it responds to you. Now, take in the energy of your suspected familiar. How is it different from the others? Some describe this bond as being similar to a soulmate connection. You just know that they have chosen you.

If you are still uncertain as to whether your pet is your familiar, try performing a little bit of spell work. This will also help facilitate contact between you and your familiar spirit. This kind of spell working is similar to the spell work that helps reveal whether your cat is your animal guide.

SPELL TO REVEAL
YOUR FAMILIAR TO YOU

Perform this spell if you want or need to find your familiar.

You Will Need:
- A black candle
- Lighter

Spell Working:
1. Have the candle on your altar or in a personal sacred space.
2. Cast a circle.
3. Light the candle.
4. Intone the following invocation three times:

> *If it's truly meant to be*
> *And you are to work with me*
> *Oh, familiar spirit*
> *This is my call, so hear it*
> *It is time for your reveal*
> *Let the magic be our seal.*
> (after the third time)
> *So mote it be.*

5. Continue to watch the flame of the candle.
6. Take note if your pet enters the room or if you see one in your mind's eye.
7. If nothing showed up for you during this working, let the candle burn for another ten minutes, then snuff it out. To continue the working, relight and burn the candle for the next two nights (a total of three nights). Use the chant each time.
8. Open the circle.

Tip: Pay attention to your dreams over the next few nights to see whether an animal makes an appearance. If there are any candle remains, leave them on the altar until you're sure of the spell's outcome, then dispose of it.

So, now that we know what guides and familiars are, and how to recognize them, how do they differ? What roles do they truly play in our lives? How can we connect with them on an energetic level? One of the main differences begins right in the very definition of what they are, not only in relation to us, but also in power and overall energetic makeup. Their roles in our lives may vary depending on what we need them to be.

As mentioned before, guides can exist in corporeal form or solely in the astral or other metaphysical planes. A person may also have a pet as their guide that passes over the Rainbow Bridge and then their spirit stays with them to continue to guide them. Familiars too can exist in the physical or metaphysical plane. While a guide spirit can choose to remain with someone for the rest of their natural life, a familiar spirit can choose to reincarnate and come back again and again, even coming back in their witch's next life if they are once again a spiritual person, witch, or shaman.

Anyone can have an animal guide, be it a cat, dog, bird, bear, wolf, lizard, dolphin, or any other animal, even if they are not aware of them. Some people even have multiple animal guides. This is especially common among spiritual/magical peoples. However, only witches, shamans, and other magical people have a familiar, and they can only have one at any given time. There are some stories of a person having one familiar in their younger life and then a different familiar spirit in their older life. This is not the same as the familiar spirit reincarnating in a different form. It is a completely different entity altogether. This could be an example of how the energetic or magical needs of the witch change over time and the need for a different type of

power that comes with each familiar spirit.

If you have not yet established that you have an animal guide and/or a familiar with spell work, then it is advised that you do so before trying to truly connect or bond with them. Once the presence of a guide has been established, you can connect and bond with them through meditations or a Lower World shamanic journey if they do not have a corporeal form (see page 104 for the guided journey). If the guide shows up as an animal that frequents the area around your home or as a pet, talking to them—or in the case of a pet, taking care of them—can help you bond with them. Speaking to them establishes that you are open to communication. Ask them questions like you might another person, such as "How was your day?" or "Tell me about what was going on in the house today." Don't be surprised when you start getting impressions about their feelings, images that show up in your mind, or even actual words that come into your thoughts that are not your own. This is their way of speaking with you.

Even though the bond with one's familiar involves taking care of them, the bond is really forged and strengthened through magical workings. Any time you are working a spell or doing a ritual, have them in the room with you, if possible. If you are outside, you might be able to use a harness or leash to have them with you, or keep them in their pet carrier as long as this does not distress them. It is advised to wait until the animal reaches adulthood before consciously pulling on their magic or asking them to lend it. This is just for the safety of the animal form that is the vessel for the familiar spirit, as they are still growing and that requires a significant amount of energy. The bond with a familiar that exists solely on the astral plane is also established through magical workings.

While it is more common to have a familiar spirit that comes to the witch in its corporeal form as a pet, remember that they can also show up as a stray that comes and goes as they choose, appearing every few days, syncing with moon cycles, or when magic is afoot. One witch even noted a raccoon familiar that comes to their porch every evening to hang out. If this is the case, it is up to the witch to respect the boundaries that their familiar is setting. It is believed that the entities that are familiar spirits come as stray animals when it is their first time coming out of the astral or other metaphysical realms. It is an adjustment for them being in physical form and they may find it difficult to stay in one place for long periods of time. You can still bond with them in the same way—taking care of them by leaving out food and water, maybe making a small shelter with a blanket, and talking to them when they are around. If they will allow it, you can let them in for a bit while you do magical workings. However, these types of familiars will generally be more comfortable with outdoor rituals and spell work.

Animal guides and familiars that exist only in the metaphysical realm can also make appearances in the physical world. This can come in the form of stray animals showing up on your porch or even outside your workplace. How will you know whether this is more than just a stray animal? Open yourself up and feel it. Have you asked for something of your guide or familiar recently? Have you been seeking guidance or the answer to a problem or question? If yes, then this is likely their way of bringing that message or coming to your aid. Another possible form they may take is that of a wild animal. Try making a trip to a local zoo. There are stories of a lion or gorilla coming up to the glass of their enclosure and staring intently at a person, or elephants that come as close as possible, waving their trunks to get your attention. Don't discount these types of encounters if they happen. Again, be open and listen.

When shamans talk about calling upon a power animal, this is the apex of their medicine. They are not mere messengers. They are bringing the greatest lessons and healing that an animal can offer. A power animal won't ask you; they will tell you. A power animal will often herald great change in one's life. If they are coming to you as a power animal, know that serious work is just around the corner. They will demand to be heard, but they will also guide you in what they are there to teach you or how to heal.

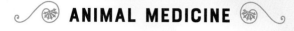 ANIMAL MEDICINE

What is animal medicine? In its most pure, basic form, it is the essence of each animal that comes forth with lessons and healing. The "medicine" is what one gains as the animal aids in helping to heal mind, body, and spirit. These animal medicine teachings have been handed down through generations of Indigenous peoples across the globe, sharing them and making them known and available to those willing to listen and learn. Each Indigenous culture works with the animals that are relevant to their area. This does not mean that they cannot learn animal medicine from those in other regions and countries as well. Because animal medicine is strong and powerful, it is no wonder that witches, shamans, healers, and other magical people seek to learn it and use it in their practices.

ANIMAL MEDICINE FOR SPIRITUAL GROWTH

Our spiritual growth within each lifetime is what teaches and nurtures our soul. Our guides and familiars come into our lives to help us in this regard. We can also use the medicine of the other animals for targeted spiritual development. The first step is figuring out what your soul is in need of at the moment.

A simple spell invoking animal energy may help you find the answer. Once you have the information, a ritual can be performed to use this knowledge and the animal medicine that aligns with it.

MEDITATION SPELL TO SEEK SPIRITUAL GROWTH LESSON

Use this meditation to find what your soul needs for spiritual growth.

You Will Need:
- A purple candle
- Cauldron or fireproof dish
- Mugwort to burn (a teaspoon amount is plenty)
- Clear alcohol to help herbs burn (Everclear burns cleanest without extra smoke or smell)
- Lighter
- Timer (it is acceptable to set a timer on your phone)
- Journal and pen

Spell Working:
1. Place the candle, cauldron, and mugwort on your altar or in your sacred space.
2. Cast a circle.
3. Light the candle.
4. Pour a small amount of the alcohol into the cauldron.
5. Sprinkle in the mugwort, light it with the lighter, and let burn. (Note: Be careful when working with fire, taking the necessary precautions.)
6. Intone the following:

> Animal medicine for spiritual growth
> Guide me and give your oath
> To show me what I must address
> Help to gain knowledge without duress
> Let me see what my soul is seeking
> I pledge to listen while you are speaking.

7. Set the timer for ten to fifteen minutes.

8. Close your eyes and begin the meditation.

9. Once the timer goes off, ground and center yourself.

10. In your journal, write down any messages you received, particularly regarding what needs to be done for your soul growth.

11. Open the circle.

Note: Make sure all fire is out.

ANIMAL MEDICINE FOR SOUL GROWTH

Once you know what you need to work on, you can decide how to go about it. One way to do that is through ritual. Using spell timing such as working with lunar and solar energies is a wonderful way to facilitate soul growth and healing. Days of the week also correspond to different energies. Call upon the animals that are associated with the respective magics. In these aspects, animal medicine is showing us how timing can affect our plan of action.

For example, if part of your spiritual work is to become a better leader and grow your communication skills, working with lion medicine on a Wednesday (the day of Mercury for communication) would be most effective. Is your magic part of how you need to grow spiritually? If you have a familiar, ask them for their medicine to help you in a working best performed on a Monday. If you do not have one, try calling upon the raven to help you open up to the magic.

ANIMAL MEDICINE FOR SPIRITUAL AND EMOTIONAL HEALING

One of the bravest things we can do is dive into our own spiritual and emotional healing. Many times we have spiritual or energetic issues going on that begin to manifest as physical issues within our bodies. When we begin to take control of our spiritual and emotional well-being, it has a ripple effect throughout our body and then our life. We see these effects in our home, in our relationships, and in how we function in society.

Invoking the medicine that an animal has to offer for healing will be a powerful ally for you. Remember that animal medicine can help us:

- Be more self-aware

- Communicate more effectively

- Work better with others

- Ground and center ourselves as well as create calmer inner workings

- Clear out heavy energies

- Set and maintain healthy boundaries

- Balance work and play and enjoy life

- Cast out self-doubt and trust ourselves, our intuition, and our instincts

- Dive into shadow work

- Cope with and heal from trauma

- Relieve stress

- Find our life path and guide us on the journey

Sometimes we need to call upon animal medicine; other times, it shows up for us by way of messages and guides. Be open to what is showing up for you.

Spell for Healing
with Animal Medicine

Use this spell to invoke an animal's medicine for healing.

Note: Be open to the animal that shows up for you. You are calling out into the Universe and you must trust that the animal that shows up is the one that you need most in that moment. If you have already received messages about which animal you need to work with, substitute the specific type of animal in the first line of the invocation for the more general "animal."

You Will Need:

- A white candle

- Cauldron or fireproof dish

- One or two small pieces of paper and a pen

- Lighter

Spell Working:

1. Find a comfortable place to sit where you will not be disturbed, such as your sacred space.

2. Set the white candle and the cauldron on your altar.

3. Cast a circle.

4. Write out on the strip of paper what needs to be healed (keep this to one or two things at a time so as not to be overwhelmed).

5. Light your candle and intone the following one time:

> *Animal medicine, I call to you*
> *We have this work to do*
> *Healing energy is what I need*
> *Bring to me with gentle speed*
> *Whether mind, body, or spirit*
> *Animal medicine here to heal it.*

6. Say out loud what is written on the paper.

7. Light the paper and drop it into the cauldron.

8. Say the chant twice more (total of three times) and then say, "So mote it be."

9. If any animal in particular showed up for you, thank them for their assistance.

10. Make sure the paper burns up completely. As always, be careful when working with open flames.

11. Open the circle.

12. Dispose of the spell ash off of your property.

Remember that healing work can be difficult, so be gentle with yourself. Be aware of what is coming up for you over the next few weeks. You can continue to light a white candle every week and intone the chant three times until you feel that it has taken hold. Also be aware that what you feel like you need to be working on isn't always what you need at that very moment. Trust that the animal medicine that is coming through to you is what you are in need of.

If you are doing healing work for others, this spell is easy to apply to them as well.

ANIMAL MEDICINE FOR RITUAL WORK
AND HEALING

The healing spell on page 58 can also be incorporated into ritual work, again taking the moon phases and days of the week into consideration. Because rituals tend to be longer than a quick circle cast and incantation, they aren't something you would want to do in a pinch. However, they can be a wonderful option for deep-seated issues that may need a little more work. This can be true of trauma and issues surrounding familial or societal conditioning.

You will find that invoking animal medicine into your ritual work is beautiful, and also a very intimate and personal thing. Working with animals that have lunar ties may bring up strong emotional aspects for an individual. This is okay. This simply means that there is work to be done there and the healing is beginning to take place. After all, the first step in healing is to acknowledge that there is an issue. The animal medicine will allow you to feel these emotions, learn where they are coming from, and help you address them in the most effective way. Be aware, though, that sometimes animal medicine is not as gentle as we would wish it to be. Sometimes healing means ripping off the Band-Aid and examining the wound. Being in ritual when animal medicine is invoked can leave one feeling raw and exposed, but know this: it will not abandon you to yourself. The animal medicine energy will stay with you as long as you need it for continued healing.

Working with animal energy is a powerful experience. They come to us with messages, offer guidance and support, lend us power, and facilitate growth and healing. There is almost no limit to how we can incorporate their magic into our practices. Being aware that they are there to help is one of the first steps we can take on the journey. Pay attention. Listen. Be open. Remember that they often know more than we do about what is needed and that is why they are coming to us. Trust the process. Trust the magic.

The "Nature" of Animal Magic

Animals are often considered synonymous with nature. They are an integral part of our ecosystem and the natural environment needs them to thrive. Without the bee, or in some cases, the fly and the bat, the plants would not get pollinated and could very well cease to exist. Some marine life helps keep kelp fields in check by feeding on it, thus maintaining a healthy balance of it in the ocean. Beavers play a significant role in the health of the rivers, and their dams can help prevent massive flooding. There are also checks and balances in nature. Bats, birds, amphibians, reptiles, spiders, and other animals feed on insects and help keep the population under control. Because apex predators like wolves and the big cats keep the ungulate (hooved animals such as deer and gazelle) numbers from getting too large, they are helping to ensure that areas are not overgrazed, which can lead to massive plant loss and erosion. There is a cycle of life in nature, and animals are a huge part of this. When food chains are disrupted, such as the loss of a major apex predator in an area, the consequences are numerous and sometimes quite disastrous.

Even without their magical attributes, animals have so much to teach us. They show us how to live in harmony with one another and our environment. Animals remind us that hard work pays off and that we also need time for rest. They can show us how to conserve our energy and also when we need those bursts of speed or adrenaline. Animals can teach us moderation and that taking too much of anything can be harmful and out of sync with the natural ways of things. They show us how important it is to preserve our ecosystems so that we may all thrive and what can happen when things are out of balance. They remind us that while we need our alone time, we must also come together in community.

All this was mentioned to show you just how impactful animals can be. Imagine harnessing this and being able to bring it into your magical practice. Just like we witches call upon the power of the moon for our rituals and spell work, we also need the energy of nature. Again, animals are an integral part of nature. Working with natural magic is often called "green magic" or "green witchcraft." This type of magic incorporates all that nature encompasses: trees, plants and herbs, stones and crystals, animals and their energy, and the elements of earth, air, fire, and water. There is a respect for the natural world and all that it holds. Working with these energies can provide a witch with incredible wisdom and knowledge and add an extraordinary amount of power to rituals and spells.

✦ ANIMALS AND THE ELEMENTS ✦

The elements are ever-present in magic. The pentagram, or five-pointed star, is a representation of the four elements of earth, air, fire, and water, and the fifth point is for Spirit. When we set up an altar, we often place representations of each of the four elements on it. We might also call upon each of the elements when we are casting a magic circle. Witches have assigned the elements to the cardinal directions of north, east, south, and west because the attributes of the elements align with the energies of those directions. Herbs, plants, and trees also have energies that correspond to each of the elements. Like the directions and the plant kingdom, animals are also aligned with the elements. Most animals have a definite element that they correspond with, but some of them vibrate with energies or have attributes that link them to more than one of the elements. To better understand how and why animals correspond to the elements, it's important to learn the characteristics of each element.

The element of earth is traditionally assigned to the north. This energy is very grounding and also healing. It is slow and steady and teaches us about stability. It relates to our physical body. The earth element is also nurturing and protective. This element is a link to the divine feminine. There's a reason we say "Mother Earth." Earth energy is life. It's renewing and regenerative. Because of its ties to the divine feminine, earth energy aligns with that of the goddess and our primordial mother. Working with this energy and animals that correspond to the element of earth can help us heal mother wounds and also balance the divine feminine within us. No matter how one identifies as far as gender, gender fluidity, or nonbinary, we are all made up of divine feminine and divine masculine energies, and this is in no way linked to your personal identity.

Within our own bodies, the root chakra vibrates with earth energy. This chakra is the foundation for our energetic body and all the other chakras. This foundation includes everything we need to thrive and feel safe in life, such as food, water, shelter, and emotional well-being.

Because of the grounding and steady energy of the earth element, we find that it is some of the larger animals that are aligned with it. Most of us have heard the term "mama bear" and it is typically associated with the highly protective instinct of a mother over her children. Yes, mother bears are known for being aggressively protective of their cubs, but so are numerous other animals. Perhaps this term also aligns with the protective energies of the earth, to which the bear corresponds. These large mammals lumber about in search of food, slow and steady, but just like a tremor during an earthquake, the bear can react with sudden speed and power. Bears are known to hibernate in a den that is either dug into the earth or in a cave, absorbing the energy of Mother Earth during their winter slumber, furthering their connection to this element.

The mighty elephant is also tied to the earth element as well as the root chakra. The largest of the land mammals wander their territories in matriarchal family groups, linking them to the divine feminine and the goddess. All the adult members of the herd nurture and protect the young. In many cultures, elephants represent prosperity and vitality, two characteristics of earth energy. Wisdom is probably one of the most well-known elephant traits. What is the earth but a vast vault of wisdom with our history written in the bedrock and the rings of the trees?

Bison are another representative of the earth element. These grazers of the plains can show us what strength and perseverance mean. The large hump that supports their massive head is what gives them the power to move snow out of the way to not only walk through, but also to find food beneath it. Many of us have seen the iconic images of the Yellowstone bison in the winter with their coat crusted over with snow and ice. This is what it means to persevere. Earth energy is this strength, this ability to go the distance and withstand the harshness that life can dole out. A herd of bison and their stampede shakes the ground and can be heard for miles. This is what it means to come together, to bring the power of the earth. It's the ability to adapt to what is going on around us, just like the bison. Native Americans revere the bison as an animal that can show us how to walk our sacred path upon Mother Earth.

ANIMALS AND THE AIR ELEMENT

The element of air usually represents the direction of east. This is a place of beginnings, like the rising sun. The element of air facilitates communication and delivers messages. It is considered the element of intellect. Air is the one natural element that is invisible. We cannot see it, yet it is responsible for movement, for flow. Air is our breath and is vital to life. It's the expansion of our lungs and the oxygen in our blood. The element of air is both life and destruction. It can be a gentle breeze that rustles the leaves in the trees or a violent howling that rips those same trees from the ground. In this aspect, air teaches us that our words have power. We can use them to nurture or to destroy another. The element of air is associated with the divine masculine.

Our heart chakra is tied to the element of air and some would argue that our throat chakra is as well because it is how we communicate. We do communicate through our hearts and it is known as an intelligent organ. We often ask whether someone is thinking with their heart or their head. The heart chakra's position within our body also envelops the area of our lungs.

It's easy to see why birds are associated with air. They of course rely on it and its currents to take flight. Birds are also known messengers of Spirit, especially hawks, eagles, and owls. While Christianity links the heavens to their god, pagans and witches tie it to the Universe and the world of Spirit. When these animals soar into the sky, they are part of the heavens and closest to that world. It is here that they accept the duty to deliver messages to us. Bird feathers have long been collected as symbols of the skies; various types and colors are believed to deliver different kinds of messages. Before we invented the ink pen, we used quills made from bird feathers to write out our communications. Certain birds, such as ravens, are known for their keen intellect; others, like parrots, are able to mimic our speech as well as use those words in an intelligent manner. The blue-throated hummingbird as well as bluebirds and blue jays are associated with the throat chakra.

A lot of flying insects such as the dragonfly are associated with the element of air. Dragonflies are known metaphysically for their ability to help us communicate with the world of fae. These colorful little creatures remind us that there is joy in the lightness of being. They also help us take flight into the deeper meaning of life and self-realization.

One normally wouldn't associate the deer with the air element, but because their antlers reach up toward the heavens, they facilitate communication with the Universe and Spirit. Deer are also known for being active early in the morning, with the rising sun, linking them to the direction of the east and, through that, the air element. Seeing fawns in the forest is one of the signs of spring, the season associated with the eastern direction. The antelope is the animal associated with the heart chakra.

ANIMALS AND THE FIRE ELEMENT

The element of fire is tied to the direction of the south. Fire is known for its transformative nature. It's the spark of life. Fire gives us passion and desire, creativity and free-form thinking. It is light and warmth. This energy sparks change, and through that change, growth. It allows us to shed what no longer serves us. When early humans learned to harness the power of fire, our lives changed for the better. However, fire is also to be respected because as much as it helps us, it can also be highly destructive. Some would argue that the destructive nature of fire cannot be seen as a good thing; however, we often need to burn things down before we can rebuild them. Some trees, such as the lodgepole pine and eucalyptus, have seeds that can only be released through fire. This element is associated with divine masculine energy.

The solar plexus chakra is aligned with fire energy. This is the seat of our personal power. We talk about feeling "the fire in our belly," and this means what drives us—passion, excitement, and determination. The ram, which is the astrological animal assigned to the fire sign Aries, is linked to the solar plexus.

The animal that most often comes to mind when we think of transformative energy is the snake. The snake sheds its skin in order to renew its protective scales and grow. Shedding is also a means to remove harmful parasites. Because of this, the snake is aligned with the power of fire. Like other reptiles, snakes are cold-blooded animals and need the warmth of the sun to heat their blood. This links the snake to the life-sustaining energies of fire through the sun. We might also think of venomous snakes and the fire in their bite. Again, we see the destructive fire energy as well as its healing properties. Snake venom can easily be fatal, but it is also being used in medicine to treat and heal. Certain venoms are known anticoagulants and can be used to treat blood clots and other coagulopathy issues. On the opposite end of the spectrum, some venoms cause the blood to clot quickly and are being used in medicine to help with homeostasis when quick clotting is necessary. Although there are some that do not adhere to this "rule," venomous snakes are often identified by their triangular-shaped head. We can associate this with the element of fire in the "fire triangle" of oxygen, heat, and fuel, which tells us what fire needs to thrive.

Another animal linked to fire through its venom is the scorpion. Although scorpions can be found in a multitude of habitats, they are most often found in deserts or semi-arid climates. The heat of the desert and the scorching sun link scorpions to the element of fire. The stinger of a scorpion is a triangular shape, thus tying it to the fire triangle.

The animal that has immense solar energy is the lion. Lions adapt to the heat of the African savannahs and their golden hue makes them synonymous with the power of the sun. The mane of an adult male lion is thought to be representative of the solar corona, the part of the sun that extends outward into the Universe, radiating powerful energy. One attribute of fire not previously mentioned is courage, and when it comes to this, lion is the animal that typically comes to mind. Lion energy is also the wilder nature of fire, a force to be reckoned with. The power of the lion reminds us of our own unique power and gives us the ability to move forward with passion.

Water is the element that is assigned to the direction of the west. It is deeply tied to our emotions. Water energy can be calm and rejuvenating, but it can also be wild. It is free-flowing and has the power to change the landscape over time, as seen in the canyons and the carving of glacial lakes in the mountains. Water is often referred to as the nectar of life because without it, we cannot survive. While it is necessary to sustain life, it can also be highly destructive. Water holds the energy of balance. Too much water means flooding and too little makes it hard to survive. Shallow waters dry up quickly and the deep waters are too cold to sustain most life. This element is tied to the moon, and because of that, the divine feminine and the goddess. With the moon ruling the tides, water is teaching us that life is cyclical and flows from one state into another.

Water is tied to our sacral chakra. This chakra is associated with sensuality, intimacy, empathy, self-esteem, confidence, and self-love. Because water rules our emotions, it isn't difficult to see why it is aligned with the sacral chakra.

We would naturally think of water-dwelling animals when it comes to those associated with this element. Clams and oysters remind us that it is sometimes necessary to close ourselves off to certain emotions. The whale that dives deep holds the energy of resurfacing after shadow work, reminding us to take a breath when we are done before moving forward again. They also show us that communicating our emotions to those around us, mainly close relations such as our friends and family, is vital to our overall health. The "cleaner fish," such as remora and plecostomus, show us how to live in harmony with others and also that the energy of water is cleansing and healing. Fish in general are associated with the sacral chakra. Fish live in communities or can be solitary animals. There is benefit to both of these scenarios. Fish aquariums have long been revered for their ability to bring calm to an individual gazing upon it.

Cranes and herons are birds that live near the water and rely on it as their source of food. While these large avians can fly, because they need the water to survive, they are associated with this element. Both of these animals teach us the importance of patience and the need to move at the right moment to gain what is needed. Cranes are symbols of tranquility. An image of a still, quiet lake with the sun setting on the horizon, the crane standing at the water's edge, comes to mind. Herons also hold tranquil energy and symbolize meditation and self-confidence.

The wild, free-flowing energy of water is represented by the horse. This is not a likely association that comes to mind, but because the horse is a symbol of freedom, endurance, and confidence, it is linked to the water element. Like the river that flows, wild and untamed, from the mountains to the sea, letting nothing stand in its way, the horse also travels on, jumping obstacles and cutting quickly to avoid others. There are also a couple of proverbs that relate horses to water, such as "Drink from the water where your horse drinks, for they will not drink bad water" and "You can lead a horse to water but you cannot make it drink." Both of these hold their own value. Our emotions or the emotions of others can be toxic and if a horse wouldn't "drink" that, then neither should we. The second proverb can relate to the stubborn nature of water and that it will do what it wants to, go where it wants to, much like the freedom-loving energy of the horse. Because the sun sets in the west, this direction is linked to death and it is said that death rides upon a pale horse.

⚘ WILD ANIMAL MAGIC ⚘

ncountering animals in the wild can be an amazing and awe-inspiring experience. It can also be a bit frightening at times. Wild animals can be unpredictable. While it is never advisable to approach a wild animal, that does not mean that you cannot enjoy the experience if you give them plenty of space and they are not acting in an aggressive manner.

As mentioned in the "Understanding Animal Energy" chapter, we sometimes have encounters with animals in their natural habitat because they are coming to us with a message or to offer some guidance. This might be a particular animal guide manifesting in a physical form to deliver the information. An example is someone who has a moose as an animal guide and while out hiking in the mountains of Colorado, a large bull moose walks onto the trail in front of them. The moose looks at them, and suddenly that person gains answers or knowledge that they need.

Other possibilities for animal messages in the wild is a direct message from a deity or the Universe being delivered by a particular animal. One example is a doe wandering into your campsite and knowing she was sent by the goddess Artemis. You hear the words of the goddess as you gaze upon the doe, and now know how to proceed with something that has been puzzling you regarding a moon ritual. Maybe while on an African safari, a bull elephant passes the caravan and when he does, you feel the presence of the Hindu god Ganesh. The elephant makes eye contact with you as he turns his massive head, and in that moment, clarity is gained and you know that the god will help you remove obstacles that stand in your way.

When Spirit or the Universe relies on wild animals to send messages, it might come across in several ways. Sometimes it might be an animal you like or resonate with. It could be an animal whose energy aligns with the message being delivered. Other times it might be one that Spirit or the Universe knows you will not ignore. If you spot a bear down the trail, it is highly likely that you will take notice. The message comes across loud and clear that you have things you need to heal and that when it is time to rest, you need to make sure that you do so. The bear wanders off, having delivered her message, and you are left knowing that Spirit has spoken.

We can sometimes gain these messages or insights from things that are directly associated with the animal, but not the animal itself. For instance, bunny tracks in the snow might bring a message to be in tune with your environment and that the need to act quickly may arise. An empty bird's nest you find at a rest spot on your favorite hiking trail might let you know that there are things that need to be done around your own home to make it more comfortable or functional. A shed snakeskin found while wandering near your campsite could be there as a reminder that it is time to shed what is no longer serving you so that you can grow.

While a lot of encounters with wildlife are simply animals living their lives in their natural habitat, some of them are purposefully seeking you out so they can deliver their message. It is important not to discount any messages, impressions, or visions that come across during these encounters.

TAKE A WALK ON THE WILD SIDE RITUAL

This simple ritual is designed to help you get in touch with your wild side so that you may get better acquainted with what it feels like to receive messages from wild animals.

You Will Need:

- Altar or sacred space with room to dance around

- One black candle and one orange candle (these represent the colors of a tiger, which is known for its wild and primal energy)

- Lighter

- Figurines or images of wild animals, feathers, or wearable animal prints

- Jungle or wild animal sounds to listen to

- Journal or paper and a pen. (You can document this in your Book of Shadows if you have one instead of a journal, if that's what you feel called to do.)

Spell Working:

1. Go to your sacred space.

2. Place the candles, lighter, and figurines/images in the space along with the device for listening to the jungle sounds.

3. Cast a circle.

4. Begin playing the jungle/wild animal sounds.

5. Light the black and orange candles.

6. Lifting your hands upward, ask that if there are any wild animals that wish to join you or have messages for you, they may do so within the space and time of this ritual.

7. Begin to dance, letting the wild, primal energy fill you, infusing you with the feelings of freedom and the glory of nature. Do not worry about what this might look like to others; this dance is meant to be wild and unchoreographed.

8. Dance until you feel the time is right to stop, when you feel that wild energy bubble up inside you and around you.

9. Take a moment to write down how this wild energy made you feel. Note any emotions, images, or messages that came through.

10. Let the candles burn down completely, making sure all fire is out.

11. Stop the jungle/animal sounds.

12. Thank any animals that showed up during this time.

13. Open the circle.

✺ DOMESTICATED ANIMAL MAGIC ✺

I t is believed that humans first began domesticating animals around ten thousand years ago, most likely with the goat first, then quickly followed by the sheep. There is debate that our canine pals were domesticated much earlier, anywhere from fourteen thousand to twenty-nine thousand years ago somewhere in northern Eurasia. Many of the animals we have chosen to work with are either to make our lives easier in some way or as a source of food. Even dogs and cats initially served as a benefit to us rather than being our adorable companions.

CATS

Cats were originally believed to have been domesticated by the Egyptians around thirty-five hundred years ago, but more recent evidence suggests that they were first domesticated in the Fertile Crescent region with the rise of agriculture around ten thousand years ago.

Our sassy little companions have come a long way since then, but their energy remains the same. Domestic cats, regardless of their gender, align with the divine feminine and the goddess. Their vibrations also sync with those of the moon. This innately ties them to the mystical and the magical. Cats make the perfect companion during rituals or while doing other magical workings.

Cats are quite clever and resourceful and have many lessons to teach us. They represent the need for independence and being able to do things on your own terms. If you struggle in this area, calling upon the energy of the cat would be a benefit for you. They also have lessons regarding rest and play. While domesticated cats kept in a home no longer need to hunt for their food, they take guarding their home and its energy seriously. Some cats are still avid mousers, but the energetic balance of the home is now their main job, and they do it well. However, they still take time to rest and play, reminding us that we too must care for ourselves in this way. A cat's grooming is also a reminder that a little self-care is always a good idea.

INVOCATION FOR CAT ENERGY

- Use this invocation to call upon the energy of a domestic cat.

- Light a black candle (corresponds with magic and mystery) and say:

Feline friend
Curious and independent
Show me your clever ways
Teachings of resourcefulness
And healer of the spirit
Please join me on this day.

CHICKENS

These feathered friends that we rely on as a source of eggs are another of the oldest animals to be domesticated, seven to ten thousand years ago in Southeast Asia. Chickens with white earlobes tend to produce white eggs while those with red earlobes produce brown eggs.

Because chickens produce eggs, a symbol of fertility and life, the animal itself also holds that energy. The quandary of "What came first, the chicken or the egg?" leads us in a never-ending debate, and because of this, the chicken also represents infinity or eternal life.

Chickens are loud creatures, especially in numbers and if there is a rooster present. These animals can remind us that it is important to find your voice and not let it get lost in the crowd. Chickens also have a very pronounced strut, for they simply do not just walk. They can also boast bright colors, particularly the roosters. The energy surrounding this tells us that we should be our own unique selves and be proud of who we are. Don't be afraid to stand out. However, it is also a reminder that we do not want to engage in the shadow aspect and become too proud or arrogant.

Chickens may also represent a lack of or need for courage in your life. The taunt of "being a chicken" when it comes to situations is representative of this. It also means that we need to take a look at the scenario and decide whether moving forward would be worth any potential sacrifice that may arise because of that decision.

Invocation for Chicken Energy

....

- Use this invocation to call upon the energy of the chicken.

- Light a white candle (corresponds to moon energy and the egg) and say:

The warmth of your feathers
Protect nestled eggs
A symbol of fertility and life
Letting your voice be heard
I ask the chicken to show me how.

⚼— COWS —⚼

Cows are believed to have been domesticated around ten thousand years ago from the now-extinct auroch, an ancient bovine species that likely evolved in Asia and then migrated west and north in search of greener pastures. The first domesticated cows were kept for their meat, milk, and hides. Their cousin the ox was an asset during the rise of agriculture to help haul heavy loads and plow fields.

The cow is a link to the divine feminine and holds Mother Goddess energy. In the Hindu religion, cows are sacred because they are tied to their deities. Hathor, the Egyptian goddess of motherhood, beauty, and sensuality, is often depicted wearing a headdress of cow horns, again linking these bovines to the divine feminine. Cow energy can be used in fertility magic and can also be called in to aid with childbirth. Calling upon the cow might also help heal mother wounds and facilitate repairing a relationship with one's mother.

In relation to "greener pastures," the cow teaches the need to move on once something is no longer serving us and that better circumstances await us. Because of their ties to the Mother Goddess, Gaia, cows also represent abundance and prosperity and their energy is a powerful ally in spell work or rituals for health and wealth.

Invocation for Cow Energy

- Use this invocation to call upon the energy of the cow.

- Light a green candle (corresponds with Mother Earth) and say:

Being of Mother Earth
Divine feminine and fertile energy
Whose milk sustains life
I honor you
Your gift of abundance and prosperity
Stability and nurturing
I ask the cow to join me on this day.

DOGS

Deemed "man's best friend" for a reason, dogs are incredibly loyal. Unlike the more aloof and independent cat, dogs love to work alongside humans and be in our presence. They can teach us what it means to be loyal and devoted to others or a cause. They remind us that we too should give back and be of service to our communities.

Like the dog-headed Egyptian god, Anubis, who watches over graves and departed spirits, our canine companions can also be fierce protectors. This is a more physical protection as opposed to the cat's energetic protection. If one is in need of protection, calling upon the energy of the dog, even if you do not have one, can lend the metaphysical support you need. The protective energy of a dog can help establish wards around your home and property.

Dogs are notorious for being fun-loving and adventurous. If you need more fun and adventure, calling upon the energy of the dog can help with this. It will also lend bravery to get out and explore more.

We see a very distinct line between our canine friends and wolves, but we must not forget that all dogs are descended from wolves. We naturally think of a wolf's pack. When we bring a dog into our home and our lives, we become their pack. They can teach us what it means to be family. We might also think of a wolf's howl, and our waggy-tailed companions do this sometimes too. The howl is a way to communicate, and calling upon the energy of a dog can help facilitate better communication, particularly with our friends and loved ones.

INVOCATION FOR DOG ENERGY

- Use this invocation to call upon the energy of the dog.

- Light a brown candle (corresponds with pets and the bond we have with them) and say:

Best friend to man
Devoted and loyal
Show me your ways
Of fun and adventure
And when protection is needed
I ask you to stand guard.

⸗— HORSES —⸗

The ancestor to these majestic beasts is believed to have first made their appearance in Eastern Eurasia approximately 160,000 years ago and then was domesticated in the western area of the Eurasian Steppe around six thousand years ago. With the rise of agriculture, the horse proved to be a wonderful ally, helping to haul heavy loads and plow fields. They also became an important mode of transportation.

Because the horse has the ability to haul heavy loads, they can teach us about how to bear a heavy burden and also when it is time to stop carrying it. Their energy can be called upon to help with stamina and perseverance. Horse energy can also assist with astral travel and journey work.

As mentioned before, the energy of the horse still symbolizes being wild and free even though they have been domesticated. If you need help breaking free, call upon the horse. Let them show you how to run with the wind in your hair and embrace the wild, wide openness that lives within your heart and soul. They can also fan the flames of your competitive nature should the need arise.

INVOCATION FOR HORSE ENERGY

- Use this invocation to call upon horse energy. This invocation is different from the one in the "Understanding Animal Energy" chapter because sometimes we need to access the varying energies of that animal. Use the invocation that calls to you most in that moment because that's the one you need.

- Light a red candle (corresponds to stamina and wild, free energies) and say:

I feel the strength of the horse
I ask you to help me go the distance
With stamina and the ability to carry a load
Let your need for wild freedom
Tell me when it's time to let go
So that I may break free of the confines
That hold me back
Help me to travel safely
Wherever I need to go.

HOW ANIMALS SHAPE OUR LIVES

All animals have their own energy and can help us in some way. The ones that we have domesticated are the ones that we tend to interact with more, so their energy is more prevalent in our lives. Some of these animals are now simply our companions while others still provide food or services for us. Some animals are companions while also having jobs to do.

Dogs, for example, are one of the best companions we humans could ask for, but there are many working dogs out there. These are the herders of cattle and sheep, the protectors, and the retrievers. Dogs are support animals for those with special needs and can use their acute sense of smell to track down drugs and explosives. Some keep horses for pleasure riding but they also still provide a mode of transportation on large ranches or even for police officers in crowded downtown areas. They are also involved in the highly competitive sport of racing.

Cattle and other livestock have been bred to be an abundant food source for us. Indigenous cultures all over the world have hunted wild animals similar to our modern-day livestock, such as bison, wild boar, birds, and waterfowl. Those cultures always believed in never taking more than what was needed and always giving thanks for it. The ancient pagan beliefs were similar to this. It is still the belief of people who follow those teachings and traditions today. Shamans, Wiccans, and other pagans often say a prayer of thanks for what they consume, whether it be plant or animal. In some cultures, there is a belief that consuming a particular animal will give them some of its magic and power.

There is no doubt that animals shape our lives. Without them, we would lose some of the most important friendships in our lives as well as a prevalent source of food and assistance. Sometimes the magic they bring into our lives is subtle and other times it screams at us. When we become more aware of the fact that animals in our lives do bring messages and wisdom, we can learn to be more open to receiving it. Some may question what is to be learned from animals that have seemingly low intelligence, but there is *always* something we can gain from them.

Sheep, for example, have a herd mentality, which is where the term *sheeple* comes from, meaning that there are some people who tend to follow a crowd instead of thinking for themselves. However, a sheep grows their wool thick and fluffy for protection during the winter and then they shed it in the late spring. We now shear them for their wool. This teaches us that we must sometimes grow our defensive layer in order to protect ourselves but that we must also learn to shed it when it is no longer needed. The phrase "the black sheep of the family" reminds us that individuality is something to be proud of and that we shouldn't be one of "the sheeple," but our own unique selves.

Take time to talk to the animals in your life. See what they have to say. If you know someone who lives on a farm or ranch, see whether you can visit with some of those animals—the cows, horses, pigs, and chickens. Let them know you have come to seek their wisdom. Animals can sense when we come to them with openness, and they love to help. They appreciate it when they are not overlooked as a source of wisdom and guidance.

Pigs are often dismissed because they roll in the mud, but they are shockingly intelligent. We can learn quite a bit from them. They can tell us how to root out solutions to difficult problems as well as how to get out of mucky situations. Covering themselves in mud is actually a way to keep their sensitive skin from sunburning, reminding us that we too need to take precautions when it comes to protecting our own sensitive nature.

Let go of all preconceived notions about what each animal means in terms of society. To many, a cow is just meat and milk, but they, like all animals, are so much more. Animals see, feel, and think way more than we tend to give them credit for. They are sentient beings, and most magical and spiritual people believe that they too have souls. Sometimes just being in their presence allows their special energies to influence us in a way we didn't know we needed. Other times they may come to us with a message or some piece of wisdom that will help us on our path. We can also call upon their magic in our practice to lend power to our workings.

By acknowledging the power of the animals and the elemental energy that they hold, we gain access to magic that would otherwise go untapped. Whether you are working with wild animal energy or that of a domesticated animal, letting them assist and guide you will be a rewarding experience.

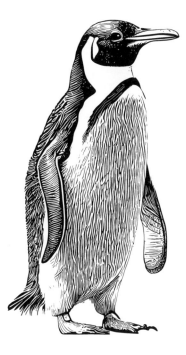

Communicating with the Animals

The word *zoolingualism* means the ability to speak with animals and understand their native language. While this word is attributed to the fictional world created in books and movies, it is possible, although rare, in reality. It means that if a squirrel is chattering at you, you can clearly understand his message. It does not involve a psychic or spiritual connection, which is the more common way to communicate with animals. The connection form of communication is a bee landing on you and you "hearing" the message that you need to enjoy the sweetness of life more.

Animals also speak to us through their energy and symbolism. With energetic communication, it leaves you feeling a certain way that might cause you to take action or evaluate things in your life. Seeing a snake shed its skin might leave you thinking how good it must be to get rid of something that has been outgrown or no longer needed, causing you to think about what you are holding on to that is no longer helping you and then letting go of negative behavior patterns. Animal symbolism can come to us in dreams or in our waking hours. Although there is plenty of information about animal symbolism in books and online, the meaning is often something very personal. If you dream of elephants, think about what they mean to you and how their energy comes across so that you can interpret what they are trying to tell you. An aggressive elephant would mean something different than a peaceful one.

It is easy to believe that communicating with animals is a difficult or cumbersome process. While speaking with and receiving messages from corporeal animals as well as those that come to you in spirit form is not complicated, there is etiquette that should be acknowledged.

COMMUNICATION ETIQUETTE

As you will quickly learn, speaking with animals is different from communicating with other types of guides or messengers. One of the most important things to remember is that we *ask*; we do not *demand*. Other than being rude, commanding that they speak with us or send us a message insinuates that we are masters over them, and this is simply untrue. Some animals, because of their ties to a particular element or their own power and magic, feel as though it is their duty to help us. Other animals that have a direct link to the Universe, Spirit, or a deity are being sent to us by that entity and they accept this role and take it seriously. Although we may ask, they are not obligated in any way to answer. Each animal exerts their own free will when it comes to communicating with us.

Animals willingly help us, and these communications need to be respected and not dismissed. When we dismiss the messages or guidance they are bringing us, we are essentially saying that we are not taking it seriously. Sometimes these messages escalate and sometimes they simply go away, leaving you to your own devices. If the bear keeps coming to you in your dreams, letting you know there is something that you need to heal and you continually ignore her, you might see that she becomes more aggressive. She might swipe her paw against the ground, snort, and act like she is charging you. This more aggressive behavior is an attempt to get you to see how important it is to listen and let her guide you to what needs to be done. When you ignore an animal message and they decide they are not getting through to you, they may leave altogether. When you next call upon them for their help, they may not show up.

OFFERINGS

Much like working with the fae, offerings to animal helpers, guides, and messengers are appropriate and appreciated. Offerings should typically be given after working with an animal. This can include asking them to help with spells and ritual work. If you ask them for messages and know that they have delivered, showing your appreciation in the form of an offering is fitting.

The type of offering depends on the animal you have been working with. Some of the offerings can be left on your altar or in the home and others should be given outside. For example, you can leave a ball of yarn on your altar for a cat guide you've been working with or you could choose to leave a bit of fish outside for them as their offering. What you might give to the animal is often something intuitive, but other times you might need to consider it in advance so that you have something appropriate for them. Here are some ideas to help you.

Carnivores are animals that eat meat; they include canines like wolves, coyotes, and dogs. All the big cats and bears are also carnivorous. Raw meat left outside is an appropriate offering for any of these animals.

Herbivores are animals that eat only plants; they include deer, cows, and elephants, so they would appreciate tender green leaves and fresh grass as an offering.

Cats (domestic or big) enjoy catnip, fish, feathers, and balls of yarn.

Dogs love tennis balls, meat, bones, or other dog treats.

Horses like oats, apples, and carrots.

Bears enjoy fish, meat, and berries.

Birds of prey, such as eagles, hawks, and owls, like raw meat but other birds prefer seeds. All birds appreciate nesting items such as bits of yarn. The corvids (ravens, crows, and magpies) also love shiny objects.

Snakes are tricky in that you cannot leave a mouse for them. They like objects that signify magic to you. Obsidian is also a good choice.

Dolphins love rubber balls and fish.

Insects appreciate foliage to be left for them to climb on or hide in, and bees and butterflies are thrilled with flowers.

Tortoises and turtles are omnivores, meaning they eat both plants and meat, such as fish, snails, and insects. Foliage, veggies such as lettuce and carrots, flowers, fruits, fish, and shrimp are all appropriate for these reptiles.

You can also offer intangible things, such as music or poetry, to any animal. Creating a song or poem for them is a wonderful way to express your gratitude for their help.

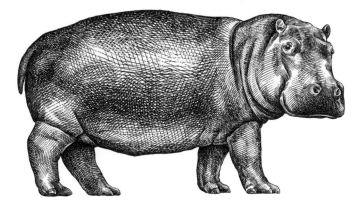

COMMUNICATING WITH ANIMAL MESSENGERS AND GUIDES

If you are unsure whether the animals that you meet or the ones in your dreams are actually messengers or guides trying to communicate with you, there are ways to make these determinations. Part of this process is determining whether animals that you come across are indeed messengers and guides, or even a familiar. Using the knowledge gained and spells in the "Understanding Animal Energy" chapter can help you with this.

Documenting encounters will help you to see whether there are any patterns. Write down each encounter that's out of the ordinary. Simply greeting a pet each day or cuddling with them is not the type of interaction that would generally need to be recorded. However, if each time you pick up your cat over a week's time you get an image of something unrelated to their care, make a note of it. A deer sighting while you're out hiking is most likely just that—a sighting—but if they pass you and then look right at you and you suddenly know the answer to a question you've been trying to figure out, record it.

Once you become more aware that animals are trying to communicate with you, it becomes easier to receive their messages. Everyone can learn to communicate with them, it just takes an open mind, an open heart, and a little practice. If you really feel that an animal is trying to get a message across to you but you just cannot grasp it, let them know you do not understand and then ask them to deliver the message in a way that you can understand. Sometimes they do not realize that we are not able to get what it is they are trying to tell us. This lets them know that we are not ignoring them—we simply do not understand.

If you struggle to hear them, or cannot seem to open up to the messages, remember you can use the spell on page 42 to open the crown chakra, which facilitates spiritual communication. Using crown chakra–opening crystals such as amethyst, fluorite, selenite, charoite, or howlite will also help. Try creating a grid with the crystals on your altar or in your sacred space to open up the channel. Remember that it is important to also set your intentions when creating a crystal grid so that the stones know what you are trying to accomplish. This is as simple as

stating that "this crystal grid is to assist with communication with animal messengers and/or guides."

If you have an animal that has been coming to you but you are not receiving the message or guidance, try using something to focus the energy. This could be a figurine of the animal or a photograph. Having a representation of the animal will help you bring that energy in so it is more concentrated, allowing it to be focused so that the message can come through. While you can keep the focus object on your altar or in your sacred space, it is better to keep it with you or have a second one that can travel with you. You could keep your wolf figurine on your altar and then download an image of one and use it as the background on your phone or work computer.

Meditation is another helpful tool when it comes to being able to receive messages. Meditation can be simply clearing your mind so that the chatter of life is out of the way, making it possible to hear the words coming from messengers and guides. You can also set intentions before going into a meditation so that your higher self, the Universe, Spirit, and any messengers or guides know what you are trying to accomplish with the meditation. You should be in a comfortable place where you won't be disturbed and have a timer you can set nearby.

MEDITATION INTENTION FOR ANIMAL COMMUNICATION

Use this incantation to set intentions for animal communication for your meditation.

1. Light a white, blue, or purple candle. White is for Spirit, blue is for communication, and purple is the color of Spirit and also the crown chakra.

2. Say the following:

> *I close my eyes and clear my mind*
> *Answers I wish to find*
> *Let me be open so I may hear*
> *Words from animals come through clear*
> *Be you messenger or guide*
> *Intentions are set and I abide.*

WORKING WITH ANIMALS IN YOUR MAGICAL PRACTICE

You are learning to communicate with the animals, now what? When we become proficient at being able to hear what they are telling us, we can begin to put those things into practice. Some of these things might involve shadow work, healing, protection magic, psychic development, divination, astral travel, and more. Animals may give us guidance when it comes to which spell or ritual we need to do as well as its timing.

To begin working with animal energy as part of your magical practice, you will need to learn what works best for you when it comes to calling upon the various animals. For animals that you have an affinity for or close relationship with, you may be able to simply bring their image into your mind and they will come. Sometimes written words work best, coming in the form of an invocation. You can create your own invocation by looking at the energies that a specific animal has and then bringing them into words with a short poem-like structure. Rhyming is fun but not necessary. Speaking from the heart about how an animal makes you feel is yet another way to call upon them and their energy.

These things work when you know which animal you need to call upon, but what if you are unsure who you need for a particular spell or ritual or at that very moment? You can use a generic animal energy call and trust that whichever animal shows up for you is the one you are meant to work with at that time.

GENERAL ANIMAL
ENERGY INVOCATION

Use this invocation when you are unsure which animal's energy you require.

1. Light a white candle.

2. Say the following:

At this moment, in this time
I call to you, asking for a sign.
Animal energy, I am in need
Your guidance I will heed
To the one that arrives
I trust that you will help me thrive.

When we bring the energy, power, and magic of the animals into our magical practice, we have access to a whole world of wisdom and knowledge that we might not have had otherwise. They can teach us things about magic and the spiritual world. They show us new things about our natural world and how to interact with it as well as how to harness other types of energy and magic. The animals can help us learn more about other people and especially more about ourselves.

If you are working a ritual or a spell, you might decide to cast a circle of protection. The circle should be cast before you call in any animal guides or energies. However, they sometimes show up as you are preparing for a ritual, anticipating your need for them. If this happens, do not worry, simply cast the circle around them. Regardless of whether you are invoking their energy or the animal is already present, make sure that you cast a wide-enough circle so that the energy doesn't feel too cramped within the barrier.

When you begin your invocation of the animal energy within
a circle, you are giving them permission to enter, thus agreeing
to the power and magic they bring as well as the delivering of
messages, visions, and whatever medicine they may have to
bestow upon you. Do not take this lightly. Also, be patient if they do
not arrive immediately. If another animal shows up in their place,
trust that this is the one that you need.

⁂ SHAMANIC LOWER WORLD JOURNEY ⁂

In the Andean shamanic tradition, the Lower World (not to be confused with the Christian hell or the Underworld in other pantheons) is where our animal guides reside. A journey means traveling into another realm or spiritual place. To journey to the Lower World, it is suggested that you record this and then play it back until you are able to journey there on your own. Drumming in the background is often found to be helpful for journey work. As with all meditations, make sure you are in a comfortable space where you feel safe and will not be disturbed. Set a timer for twenty to thirty minutes that will bring you out of the journey. Record you or someone else saying the following, and then play it back:

> Close your eyes and take three deep breaths, slowly inhaling and exhaling each one . . . Now imagine yourself in a large meadow. See the grasses moving in the breeze. You notice that there is a forest at the edge of the meadow. You begin to make your way to the trees and see a path. Follow it. The path through the trees begins to descend a little until you reach a dead end at a massive tree that reaches out in all directions. You notice a large opening at the base of the tree and that the path continues into this opening. This is the entrance to the Lower World and there is a being that guards it. You ask their permission to enter. They allow you access and point to the path that continues onward. You follow the path as it descends, down, down, down. It winds and spirals down into the earth until you reach an underground stream. You instinctively lie down in the water and let it wash over you, cleansing you. You step out again on the other side and are dry. You continue on the path until you see an opening with light spilling in. When you reach the opening, you find yourself in a beautiful world with meadows, flowers,

trees, and animals of all kinds. There is a bench waiting for you, so you take a seat. In the distance, you can see an animal approaching you. They might be just a messenger or they could be your animal guide. It is time to hear what they have to say. Remember to ask them to communicate in a way that you can understand if you are having any difficulty interpreting what they are telling you. You will stay here until you hear the timer calling you back. When you hear its call, travel back the way you came.

Take time to ground and center yourself once you are back. Then, write down your experience in your journal—any messages that come through or special guidance they had to offer you. Remember that you can make this journey anytime that you wish to.

While at first you might find communicating with animals and their energies intimidating, it can be some of the most insightful and amazing experiences of your magical and spiritual practice. With their vast wisdom and knowledge, animals have the capability to teach us things that often escape the limited vision that we might have as humans. They open up the world for us, as well as the passage to other worlds beyond what we know here in the physical realm. Be open. Let them speak to you. Let them guide you.

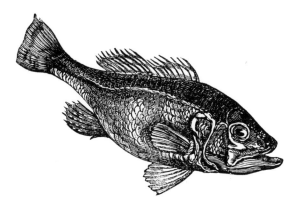

Creating Animal Enchantment in Your Life

Allowing the energies of the animals into our lives and magical practices not only lends guidance, power, wisdom, and knowledge, but it also brings with it the enchantment of the realms where these guides and messengers reside. Honoring the animals that reside in our physical world also brings magic to the mundane.

ANIMAL FESTIVALS

Cultures around the world hold festivals to celebrate various animals. Because these are so widespread, it reminds us how important these creatures are to us and our lives. Let's take a look at the celebration of animals across the globe.

TIHAR/KUKUR TIHAR (NEPAL)

The festival of Tihar in Nepal is a five-day celebration that honors animals such as cows, yaks, llamas, and crows and is held in October or November. On the second day of the festival, called Kukur Tihar, dogs are specifically honored and worshipped. This is to appease Yama, the god of death, because dogs are said to be his messengers. Worshippers may place garlands of flowers around the dogs' necks and give them offerings of meat, eggs, and dog food. Acting in a disrespectful way to a dog on this day is considered sacrilegious.

LOPBURI MONKEY BUFFET FESTIVAL (THAILAND)

This festival is held amid the ruins of the Phra Prang Sam Yot temple in Lopburi, Thailand, on the last Sunday of November in honor of the macaques, an old-world genus of monkeys that reside in this area. The festival dates back over two thousand years to the tale of the monkey king, Hanuman. He and his army helped rescue Sita, the wife of the divine prince, Rama, from the clutches of a demon. Since then, the monkeys are said to bring good luck and prosperity. A grand buffet of fruits and vegetables is set out on banquet tables for them to enjoy.

SURIN ELEPHANT ROUNDUP (THAILAND)

While the roots of the elephant roundup served as a ritual to corral and tame elephants as work animals, the modern-day festival held in Surin, Thailand, now honors the historical work of these animals' ancestors and their cultural significance in the lives of the ancient people. This celebration is held during the third week of November each year. A procession of elephants is still part of the festivities, leading them to a banquet laid out on tables consisting of thousands of pounds of fruit and vegetables.

FIESTA DE LA TRASHUMANCIA (SPAIN)

Every year in October, Fiesta de la Trashumancia takes place, celebrating the age-old tradition of the livestock migration. Oxen, bulls, cows, horses, and sheep are moved from the high country in northern Spain, through the streets of Madrid, to the more temperate region of southwest Spain, where they are wintered. Proceeding the animals, people dance and swirl in lively colors to the beat of castanets, often accompanied by tambourines and flutes. People line the streets to watch as the animals pass by, including the ceremony in which the chief herdsman pays their fee for safe passage through the city to the mayor at city hall. This ceremony dates back to medieval rule when shepherds were allowed to cut through towns and cities for an easier route with their animals.

VELAS TURTLE FESTIVAL (INDIA)

In February and March each year, approximately 143 miles from Mumbai, India, on the coast of Velas, Olive Ridley turtles, which are highly endangered, arrive to lay their eggs. Groups of volunteers stand guard over the nesting grounds so that there is no egg poaching. The hatchlings begin emerging in late March and April. The festival is about life; it's witnessing the birth of the hatchlings, and then watching them make their way to the ocean. This festival is organized by local villagers and is mostly a conservation effort.

PUSHKAR CAMEL FAIR (INDIA)

The Camel Fair in India is held each year in late October or early November. It is a cultural event that includes the trading of livestock as well as marking the Hindu pilgrimage season to Pushkar Lake. It is one of the largest camel, horse, and cattle fairs in India. Dances and competitions such as camel racing, tug-of-war, *matka phod* (the longest mustache competition), and other exhibitions are all part of the festivities. Vendor stalls are set up where handcrafted goods such as jewelry, textiles, and clothes can be purchased.

GOLDEN RETRIEVER FESTIVAL
—§— (SCOTLAND) —§—

Held each year in July at the Guisachan House in the Scottish Highlands, this festival celebrates golden retrievers. This celebration commemorates the first breeding of the goldens in 1868 at this very location by Lord Tweedmouth. Festivities include a picnic with Scottish fare, field demonstrations, and training sessions. The highlight of the festival is the dog show, where two to three hundred goldens travel from across the globe to compete. The intelligence and hardworking nature of the breed is acknowledged and celebrated.

§— BIRDS OF CHILE FESTIVAL (CHILE) —§

Each October, the annual Birds of Chile Festival is held along the country's Pacific coast, celebrating the beauty and diversity of the avians that call it home. The Andean condor, one of the largest flying birds in the world and also the national bird of Chile, can be seen by attendees. One can hear experts speak about the local birds as well as participate in bird-watching excursions.

WOOLLY WORM FESTIVAL
—§— (NORTH CAROLINA, USA) —§—

During the third week of October each year, the town of Banner Elk, North Carolina, hosts the Woolly Worm Festival. Akin to Groundhog Day, this festival uses the woolly bear caterpillar, native to the area, to forecast winter weather. Individuals sign up to enter their worm in a race and spectators cheer the worms on as they climb a length of string. The winner is the one that decides the fate of the cold season. Prize money and a trophy are awarded to the winning worm's coach.

NATIONAL LOVE YOUR PET DAY (USA)

This day falls on February 20 each year and is fairly self-explanatory. Pet lovers observe the holiday by giving their beloved pet a little extra attention and maybe even a few more treats. This day is meant to focus on the bond between humans and their pets. For those who do not have a pet, you can celebrate by donating your time to an animal rescue shelter.

NATIONAL PIG DAY (USA)

Falling on March 1, this holiday came about in 1972 when sisters Ellen Stanley and Mary Lynne Rave decided that the pig was due veneration as one of the most intelligent domestic animals. The pig, though often viewed as messy and unclean, has somehow worked its way into our hearts, with them appearing in artwork, the piggy bank, books, movies, stuffed animals, and jewelry. Since the sisters decided it was time we gave the pig its due, cities across the country plan events that include pig races, themed arts and crafts, pig parades, and even "snort off" competitions.

As you can see, people all over the world celebrate the lives of the animals and the impact they have on our lives, from a small worm to the ground-shaking elephant. Finding ways to honor them shows our appreciation for all that they are, energetically, magically, and physically. Perhaps you can have your own celebrations that align with these worldwide festivals for these amazing creatures.

ANIMAL MAGIC:  SPELLS AND RITUALS

Now we're getting to the good stuff! Here you will find invocations for animals; blessings and protection spells for pets; information on animal magic for protection, guidance, shadow work, and better sleep. There is also information and spells that include using shed items that you might find, such as fur, antlers, teeth, bones, and feathers.

ANIMAL INVOCATIONS

Remember that all animals have energy that we can work with as well as something they can teach us. To give you a wide variety of energies to call upon, the following brief descriptions of each animal's metaphysical qualities have been included along with their invocations that will help you bring that energy to you.

Bison holds strong earth energy and will show us how to walk the sacred path. She will teach you that with each step, we can align with the heartbeat of the Earth. Bison shows us what it means to be steady and carry any burden with determination and perseverance. Use this invocation to call upon the mighty bison.

Grazer of the plains
And bringer of the stampede
A sacred path upon Mother Earth
The mighty bison roams
Strength to carry the burden
Through the harsh and the cold
While honoring the gifts that
nature bestows.

Jaguar energy aligns with both the sun and the moon; however, it is divine feminine energy. She can help you see beyond the veil as she is the gatekeeper to the unknown. She helps with transitions regarding soul awakenings. Use this invocation to call upon the jaguar.

Fierce hunter of the night
With strength and grace she strikes
Jaguar, gatekeeper to the unknown
Mystic realms and awakening the soul
She sees beyond the veil
And shows one to their true self.

Moth is a symbol of the moon goddesses and can help one "see in the dark" where hidden secrets lie, helping to uncover the truth. She also helps one see the silver lining in dark situations. Use this invocation to call upon the moth.

Within the dark is where the truth lies
To the flame so bright she flies
One with the goddess of the moon
With those hidden secrets, attune
Her ability to see the light
Even on the darkest of nights
In the bleakest of times,
A silver lining moth will find.

Mountain Lion/Cougar/Puma comes to us with primal feminine energy. She brings power and grace, patience, balance, and the confidence to make the leap. She holds the energy of both the moon and the sun. Because she is most active during dusk and dawn, she can teach us how to work in the liminal spaces and use its energy.

Perched upon the craggy ledge
Her watchful golden eyes
Patience in the sacred hours
Dawn and dusk
The huntress awaits
Primal and feminine
Power and grace
Sensual and fierce
A perfect balance
Of body, mind, and spirit
Cougar stakes her claim.

Wolverine energy is fierce! He has the spirit of a warrior and will never give up the fight when he knows it matters. The wolverine can help give confidence to not back down and hold your boundaries. He shows us how to be alone when necessary to do the work that is required of us on our path, be it physical or spiritual. Use this invocation to call upon the wolverine.

Powerful and fearless
An army of one
He thrives alone
Fierce confidence
He knows no surrender
A warrior's spirit
Intense and wild
Wolverine, never to be tamed.

There are several animals that are wonderful for assisting with protection spells. These spells can be for personal protection, home and property, when traveling, or protection against spiritual and magical attacks.

PERSONAL PROTECTION

This type of spell is used for protection of your physical well-being. It is not a license to be reckless, but simply adds another layer to your smart decisions and knowing when to be cautious. The bear is a wonderful ally for personal protection and also the protection of one's children. The basic invocation for the bear can be found on page 28, but the following spell is meant to be used specifically for protection.

1. Cast a circle.

2. Light a black candle (corresponds to protection magic).

3. Bring the image of the mighty bear into your mind. See her standing her ground in front of you, wrapping you in her protective energy. You can do the same but picture her protecting your children if it is for them.

4. Say the following three times:

> *Fierce protector*
> *Bringing strength and courage*
> *Mother bear, I need you near*
> *Her mighty paws swipe the earth*
> *A signal to others*
> *That she is on guard*
> *Hear her ferocious roar*
> *Wraps around, blocking all that would harm.*
> *So mote it be!*

5. Let the candle burn out completely.

6. Thank the bear for her protection; an offering is appropriate (see page 28).

7. Open the circle knowing that bear will stay with you as long as you need her protection.

PROTECTION FOR HOME AND PROPERTY

The dog is one of the best animals to call upon for protection of your home and property. Use this spell to ask the energy of the dog to help you with protecting your home.

1. Cast a circle.

2. Light a brown candle (aligns with home protection energy).

3. See the loyal and trustworthy dog in your mind. Remember that they do not need to be vicious to project energy that will protect the home. See them walking the perimeter of your property, making sure that all is well and safe.

4. Say the following three times:

> *Best friend to man, devoted and loyal*
> *Protection is needed*
> *Scouting out what lies within our borders*
> *I ask you to stand guard*
> *Keeping out that which does not belong.*
> *So mote it be!*

5. Let the candle burn out completely.

6. Thank the dog for keeping your home and property safe. Offerings are appropriate (see page 96).

7. Open the circle.

PROTECTION WHILE TRAVELING

The horse is a wonderful option for protection while traveling. You can use the horse invocation on page 87 and the candle color listed with the following spell. Because there is strength in numbers, large animals that migrate, such as caribou (also known as reindeer), are perfect to call upon for this purpose. Use this caribou spell for protection while traveling.

1. Cast a circle.

2. Light a blue candle (corresponds to travel).

3. See the caribou in their herd, making their way across the tundra and to the grasslands, traveling the long distances while remaining alert, sticking with the herd and not wandering off into unsafe territory.

4. Say the following three times:

> *Internal compass shows the way*
> *Crossing the distance*
> *Traveling far from home*
> *Caribou gives direction*
> *Keeping safe while on the roam*
> *So mote it be!*

5. Let the candle burn down completely.

6. Thank the caribou for keeping you safe while traveling. Offerings of mushrooms, willow leaves, and grassy plants are appropriate.

7. Open the circle.

Protection Against Magical, Psychic, or Spiritual Attack

The cat is definitely an ally you can call upon if you feel you are being attacked by dark magic or on a psychic or spiritual level. They also protect against negative entities and malevolent spirits. Cats are known for their magical ability to act as a buffer against these energies and to clear it away altogether. See the basic invocation on page 31. Taking it a step further, for even more power, call upon the black panther using this spell:

1. Cast a circle.

2. Light a black candle (corresponds to protection and the black panther).

3. Close your eyes and picture a black panther stalking through the trees, deep within the shadows, waiting and watching. They feel and see the negative energy in the air and have the power to clear it all away. The black panther makes her leap and the adversary is gone.

4. Say the following three times:

> *She moves silently through the night*
> *Unseen, cloaked in darkness*
> *Stalking the prey with stealth*
> *Presence revealed only when the time is right*
> *Black panther, a force to be reckoned with*
> *Protect against magical attack*
> *Negative energy and malevolent spirits*
> *She wipes them all away.*

5. Let the candle burn out completely.

6. Thank the black panther; an offering of raw meat (outside) or catnip (inside) is appreciated.

7. Open the circle.

8. Because the candle can absorb negative energies, it is important to dispose of any candle remains off of your property, such as in a public trash can.

SPELL FOR AN ENERGY BOOST

If you are feeling sluggish and need an energetic boost, the lion is the perfect ally to call upon for this quick and easy spell. Because the lion's energy aligns with the sun, he can act as a conduit for a solar charger to assist you.

1. Stand where you can let the sunshine hit you, even if it's just through a window.

2. Light a yellow or gold candle.

3. Say the following three times:

    Do not be fooled by his napping in the sun
    Beneath the golden coat and mane untamed
    Great power lies in wait
    His connection to the hot, white light
    And the star that gives us life
    Hearing the lion's roar
    Solar energy comes my way
    Giving me the boost I need this day.
    (after the third time)
    So mote it be.

4. You can snuff the candle (do not blow it out). Wrap it in a yellow, orange, or gold piece of paper or cloth and carry it with you, continuing the energetic magic while you need it.

KOALA MAGIC
FOR SLEEP

The koala is the sleepiest of the animal kingdom, getting between twenty and twenty-two hours of shut-eye a day, making them the perfect companion to help you with a spell for good sleep. Use this spell when you have nothing left to do and it is time for bed.

1. Cast a circle.

2. Light a silver candle (corresponds to the moon and dreaming).

3. Close your eyes for a moment and see the sweet koala, dozing in their tree. Notice how peaceful they are and that they do not let the worries of the day burden them when it is time for rest. When you have them in your mind, open your eyes and say the following:

> *It's time for rest, time to sleep*
> *May my slumber be peaceful and deep*
> *Little koala, help me to unwind*
> *And clear the day's troubles from my mind*
> *Koala wraps me in calming moonlight*
> *So that I may sleep through the night*
> *I feel my eyes as they grow heavy*
> *Into my bed I will go, I am ready*
> *So mote it be.*

4. Snuff out the candle.

5. Open the circle and climb into bed.

6. Sweet dreams.

A Working for
Animal Guidance

This working is meant to call upon the animal that you need most for guidance in a particular moment. If you are trying to figure out the answer to a problem, have a big life decision to make, need guidance on your path, need insight for a specific spell or ritual, or need to know how to proceed in your magical or spiritual practice, calling upon animal energy and trusting that the right one will show up to help is what this is designed for. This is generic in nature so that it may be used in just about any situation where you are seeking guidance.

You Will Need:

- Lighter

- A blue, purple, or white candle

- A pen and several sheets of paper

- Fireproof dish

- Timer

Spell Working:

1. Cast a circle.

2. Light your candle.

3. Using the pen and paper, write out your question, what you need assistance with, or the situation you require guidance for. Be very specific.

4. Once you are done, take the piece of paper with the issue written on it and light it on fire using the lit candle. Carefully place it in the fireproof dish and allow it to burn so it is released into the Universe.

5. Say the following three times:

Animal guidance I call to you
Please show me what to do
I seek your help with this matter
It is your voice I hear above the chatter
Calm the mind so I can see
What direction is best for me.

6. Set the timer for fifteen minutes.

7. Close your eyes and think about the problem. Be open to what animal shows up for you and any messages, impressions, or visions they may bring. You have called upon them and they are here to help, so let them.

8. When the timer goes off, take a moment to write down the guidance they shared with you.

9. Make sure the paper is thoroughly burned and let the candle burn down completely.

10. Thank the animal for their assistance and give an appropriate offering (see page 96 for offerings).

11. Open the circle.

✦ ENERGY AND SHADOW WORK ✦

Deep within our souls, hidden in a faraway corner, locked down with chains behind a sealed vault door lies our shadow self. The shadow is the little parts of ourselves that we hide away, deeming them unworthy to play with others in the light. Sometimes it is a conscious choice to hide these parts away and sometimes it is not. Anything can be relegated to the shadow that we consciously or unconsciously deem inappropriate, bad, or negative about ourselves. This can be because of familial or societal conditioning, trauma, or even just our own insecurities about who we truly are.

Shadow work means taking a deep dive into that abyss. It means not only acknowledging that these darker parts of ourselves exist, but also coming to terms with them. The ideas around shadow work are beginning to change. Until more recently, the belief was that when we found these dark hidden aspects of our being, we were supposed to bring them into the light so that they were no longer dark. However, a shadow will remain a shadow, even in the light, and sometimes the light makes the shadow seem even more harsh. So instead, it seems to be more beneficial to acknowledge your darkness, embrace it, and integrate it as part of your whole being. I believe this is where the term "dancing with your demons" was coined.

Shadow work can be done through meditation, shamanic journey work, rituals, and spell work, and is especially powerful when combined with assistance from an animal guide and their power. Animal energy is a wonderful tool to use for this because animals are unapologetically themselves. They do not worry about hiding parts of themselves so that they can appease others.

There are many animals that can help with shadow work. The list includes many that are nocturnal because they are the ones that roam the darkness. Animals such as bats, scorpions, owls, racoons, and cats—including some of the big cats, especially the jaguar and black panther—can all assist you with shadow work. Some of these animals have invocations listed within the pages here. These can be altered to suit the working or you can make up your own for the animal you will be working with.

There is also the thought that shadow animals, or those that we have a fear of, such as snakes, bats, sharks, spiders, or rats, can also assist us with shadow work. Because we fear them, they bring up emotions that are often tied to something we have buried. Why do you fear the spider? Most of them are completely harmless; we pose a much greater threat to them than they do to us. Because the spider is linked to the web of fate, maybe there are some fears about your destiny? Spiders also represent the divine feminine, so there could be mother wounds that need addressing.

Energy of the Anglerfish

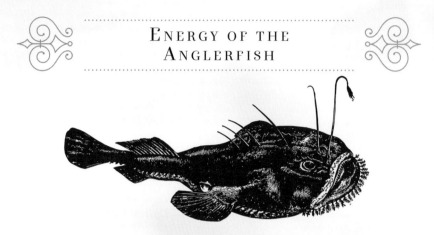

For this working, we will call upon the energy of the anglerfish. For anyone who is not familiar with this fish, it is one that lives in the depths of the ocean, in total darkness. It has a bony fin protrusion on its head that glows because of the symbiotic luminescent bacteria at the tip of this bony fin. It lights up like a lantern, attracting other fish or deep-sea creatures right to the mouth of the anglerfish.

The energy of the anglerfish represents the unseen world—in this case, the place where your shadow self resides. The anglerfish swims the depths without fear or hesitation, showing us that there is nothing to fear within our shadow. It shows you how to navigate that darkness and that there is always a light that will see you through. It is a reminder that the darkness as well as the light is part of the whole being, helping you integrate both aspects into a harmonious balance.

Note: It is always a good idea to let someone know you are diving into shadow work before proceeding with it. Notify a good friend that you trust, a family member, or a therapist who can be available once you are done. Doing this type of working is meant to bring up things that have been hidden away, and that can include trauma or abuse. Being able to speak with someone you trust about the things or emotions that came up for you can be an important part of mental health. Shadow work is meant to be a step in healing your overall being.

You Will Need:

- A picture of an anglerfish
- A white candle. a black candle, and a lighter
- A timer
- Ability to record this guided meditation
- A piece of paper and pen
- Heatproof dish you are okay with pouring candle wax into
- A clear glass jar with a lid

Spell Working:

1. Look up a picture of an anglerfish before you begin.

2. Find a comfortable, safe, quiet space. Place the black and white candles next to each other on your altar or sacred space and cast a circle.

3. Light the white candle first and say, "This is for my light." (The white candle will also promote healing.)

4. Light the black candle and say, "This is for my darkness." (The black candle can also assist with breaking bad habits.

5. Say the following three times:

   Within the deep, within the darkness
   Anglerfish I follow you, fearless
   I search for what I have hidden away
   Letting your light show me the way
   So I may find my shadows
   To lock them away is what I chose
   But now it's time to see
   The dark that is part of me
   All right here, within my soul
   As I bring together pieces to make it whole.

6. Get comfortable and set the timer for thirty minutes. Record you or someone else saying the following, and then play it back:

Close your eyes and take a deep breath. Slowly exhale. Take two more breaths. Feel yourself relax, letting go of all preconceived notions about what this is supposed to be or what will be revealed. Remember that you are safe and nothing in these shadows can harm you now.

A long, dark hallway begins to take shape. As it comes into focus, you notice a small light coming your way. It hovers there in the darkness, just about eye level. It draws closer and you begin to make out the shape of it. It is an anglerfish. While he is scary looking, you know he will not harm you. He reminds you that, like him, the shadows may seem terrifying but they are nothing to be feared. He's very close now and stops in front of you. You hear in your mind that he is telling you that you are in the halls of your mind and soul. You now notice there are doors and they are labeled. They appear to be experiences and memories, and some of them may even be from past lives. He tells you that you can visit and explore this place at any time, but for now, your destination is somewhere else.

He swims past you and you know you are meant to follow him. You continue down the hallway and then it seems to gradually descend. Suddenly he stops in front of a spiral staircase leading down. He begins to move down the staircase, so you follow. The downward spiral seems to take you into an even darker area than where you were before. Down, down, down into the black abyss you follow the anglerfish.

Finally, the staircase comes to an end and you are on solid ground again. You are in another hallway. You notice that there are no doors here except for the faint outline of one at the very end of the hall. The anglerfish continues to shine his light so that you can make your way to this door. When you are in front of it, you can see that there are several locks. The anglerfish tells you that only you can open them. You can see that they are dials that rotate, deosil and widdershins. You place your hand upon one of them and it vibrates under your touch. You instinctively know that you must turn it widdershins to unlock it. Remember, this is a counterclockwise motion that serves to unlock things. You begin to turn the dial until you hear it click. You turn the next one and then the next one and the next until they are all unlocked. You pull the lever door handle and begin to open the door. Once it is open, the anglerfish swims inside and hovers overhead, his light shining brighter than ever so that you may see what has been hidden in here. You will stay here until you hear the timer, signaling it's time to return. Remember there is nothing to fear here.

(Let twenty to twenty-five minutes play in silence on the recording.)

Now that the timer has gone off, it is time to make your way out. You have discovered what it is you needed to see and you bring it with you. It is part of you and it is meant to be brought forward. You follow the anglerfish back into the hallway, back up the spiraling staircase, until you are in the hallway of doors again. He tells you that he is happy to help you whenever you need him. He leaves you here in the hallway where you began and as he floats away, you begin to come back to yourself. Take a deep breath. Wiggle your fingers and your toes. When you are ready, open your eyes.

7. Take a moment to really come back to yourself. Make sure to write down your experience and what you saw, felt, and heard there in your shadows.

8. It is time to begin to integrate that shadow aspect.

9. Taking a piece of paper and the pen, give the shadow aspect or the experience a few key words and write them down.

10. Fold it and place it in the dish you will use for the candle wax.

11. Pick up both the black and white candles.

12. Bring that shadow aspect into your mind.

13. Very carefully, tip both candles at the same time so that their wax covers the paper, allowing it to mix. Remember that one symbolizes your light and the other your darkness and by allowing them to mix, it is facilitating the merging of the two so that you can live and walk in balance as your whole, beautiful, and marvelous self.

14. Once the paper has a significant amount of wax on it, return the candles to their holders.

15. Place your hands over the dish with the shadow aspect paper and wax and say the following:

> *My darkness and my light*
> *Both of these are right*
> *Never to be hidden again*
> *This merging I begin*
> *All a part of me*
> *My shadow, I accept you fully.*

16. Let the candles burn out completely.

17. Use the clear glass jar to store the paper and the candle wax in. It should be kept where you can see it, not hidden somewhere. If you do future shadow work this way, you can put those papers into the jar as well.

18. Thank the anglerfish for his assistance.

19. Open the circle.

Note: Please remember to talk to someone if difficult situations or emotions come up during this working.

BLESSINGS AND PROTECTION SPELLS
FOR PETS

We love our fur babies, and the scaly ones too! We take care of them and do everything we can to keep them healthy. Adding a little bit of magical protection takes it one step further. If you work with deities in your practice, calling in certain ones can add even more power to these workings. Bast, the Egyptian goddess, is purrrfect for our feline friends because she is their patron goddess and protector. Dogs are closely associated with the Greek goddess Hekate; the Celtic goddess Epona and the Celtic Welsh goddess Rhiannon are the patron goddesses of horses. Medusa may be willing to assist with snakes. Artemis, the Greek goddess of the wild, wilderness, and animals in general, can lend help for any animal. All of these blessings are meant to be generic, so that they can be used for any pet.

Pet Blessing

1. If possible, have your pet near you.

2. Cast a circle.

3. Invoke deity if you choose to and ask them to give their blessing as well.

4. Light a brown candle (corresponds to pets).

5. Say the following:

> *My dearest pet (say their name here)*
> *My friend and companion*
> *With my magic I infuse*
> *This blessing I bestow upon you*
> *May you live in health and wellness*
> *And the joyful days seem endless*
> *So bright and full of fun*
> *Until your time here is done*
> *And then your memory shall stay with me*
> *As I will, so mote it be!*

6. Let the candle burn out completely.

7. If a deity was called, thank them and bid farewell.

8. Open the circle.

PROTECTION TALISMAN FOR PETS

This spell will utilize an item the pet has on or near them at all times, such as their collar. That item will be infused with protection magic so that they carry it with them. You can use a horse's shoes. Don't worry if these items get lost or the animal outgrows it. Simply rework the spell with the new item. For animals that are in cages or a habitat, such as a bird or a snake, do the working for their enclosure.

1. Cast a circle.

2. Invoke deity if you choose to and ask them to lend their protection as well.

3. Burn a brown and black candle (for pets and protection).

4. Take the item you are using to create their talisman. Holding it in one hand with the other resting on top, say the following:

> *This (say the name of the item) I hold now*
> *Into it the power of protection I endow*
> *A barrier it shall be*
> *From harm it keeps them free*
> *(Name of the pet) is wrapped in light*
> *During the day and all through the night*
> *Safe and sound*
> *The protection spell is wound.*

5. Feel the energy of protection infusing the item.

6. Take the candles one at a time and let one drop of wax from each fall onto the item.

7. Let the wax dry on the item. If your pet is with you, you can place it on them. If your pet stays indoors, keep the wax remains somewhere inside where they cannot get to it. If the animal is a horse, you can keep the wax in the barn out of reach of them.

8. Let the candles burn down completely.

9. If a deity was called, thank them and bid farewell.

10. Open the circle.

USING FOUND ANIMAL ITEMS
IN YOUR MAGIC

Animals shed items all the time, just ask any dog or cat parent. These items, such as fur, teeth, claws, antlers, and feathers, hold the same energetic properties as the animal they came from. When people come across these shed items, such as a feather on the sidewalk, many of them believe it is a gift from that animal. If you feel it is a gift, either from the animal or Mother Nature, remember to say thank you.

We can put these items to good use, creating talismans, protection charms, spirit communication devices, and more. Remember that it is *never* okay to cut or pluck items from animals.

CREATING A FUR, HAIR, OR SHED-SKIN TALISMAN

To create a talisman, you must first decide what its purpose is. Once you know that, you can then collect or find the fur, hair, or shed skin that you need. Don't be afraid to ask friends or family members for items. If someone you know that has a snake and you need to work on letting go of what no longer serves you, ask them for a section of skin the next time the snake sheds. Or perhaps you need to regain some of your wild spirit and you have a friend who works with horses. When they brush the horse, they can collect some of its hair to bring to you.

The next step is to figure out the container you would like to use for your talisman. Many people use lockets so that the talisman is worn in public settings without attracting questions. Small glass vials with stoppers are also a good choice.

You Will Need:

- The container of your choice (e.g., locket or small glass vial with stopper)
- Incense of your choice
- Shed item that aligns with the talisman's purpose
- Candle, if using a glass vial, in the corresponding color to the spell work you are doing

Spell Working:

1. Cleanse the container of your choice with incense smoke.
2. Set the container and shed item on your altar or in your sacred space.
3. Cast a circle.
4. Pick up the container and intone the following:

   This (name the container) shall be for me
   A repository for this energy.

5. Pick up the shed item, place it in the container, and intone the following:

   The (fur, hair, or skin) of the (name animal) I place in here
   To (name the working: heal, protect, etc.)
   A talisman I create
   Working for my aid
   As I will, so mote it be.

6. If you are using a glass vial, seal it with candle wax. Using a corresponding color is recommended: black for protection, white for healing, and so on. (See pages 150 and 151 for more information on candle magic colors.)
7. Open the circle.

Tip: Use the talisman for its purpose, whether that means wearing it, placing it in the car, or gifting it to someone.

Our dogs and cats may lose teeth along the way, either shedding baby teeth or as they age. Teeth can be used for protection and defensive magic. Shed baby teeth are great for protection charms for children. If you are out on a hike and find a piece of an animal's mandible with the teeth intact, those can be used as well. Teeth from animals have long been used in spells or charm bags to help relieve toothaches. This of course does not take the place of going to the dentist. Because teeth are bones, those that "throw or read the bones" might choose to include them in their divination bag.

SPELL JAR FOR PROTECTION

Use this spell jar to create a portable protection spell. This spell jar can be left on your altar or taken wherever it is needed, such as the car or workplace.

You Will Need:
- Lighter
- Black candle
- Pen and small piece of paper
- Cleansed small jar with lid or glass vial with stopper
- Shed or found animal teeth
- Black obsidian
- Smoky quartz
- Sage (dried common garden sage is fine)
- Rosemary

Spell Working:
1. Go into your sacred space.
2. Cast a circle.
3. Light the black candle.
4. Write out exactly what the protection spell is for on the piece of paper.
5. Place all items into the jar, including the piece of paper, teeth, crystals, and herbs, and chant the following three times:

Teeth used to defend
Protect and keep safe
Herbs and stones lend their aid
Wax to seal the spell in place
(drizzle black candle wax to seal the jar)
(then, after the third time)
So mote it be!

6. Open the circle.

FINDING AND USING ANIMAL BONES

Using bones is a common practice in witchcraft. While it is not for everyone, and some may view it as morbid, using them in your magical workings is a way to honor that animal and their passing. Any found bones should be cleansed and then a few words of gratitude to them is appropriate.

Because the bones come from an animal that has passed, they can act as a conduit to the spirit world, helping you contact departed loved ones, ancestors, or even pets that have passed. The bones also hold the energy of the animal they came from, giving you a direct link to that animal's energy. Calling upon the raven may become much easier if you have a raven skull nearby. Smaller bones or bone pieces can be marked with the runic alphabet and used for divination. Long bones (those that come from the legs) of animals such as deer or elk have been used as magical staffs. Shorter bones have been used as part of wands for healing work, divination, or giving death rights to those who are about to pass.

Antlers are also bone, so found antlers can be used for these purposes. However, the energy surrounding antlers is also one of connection to the Universe and Spirit. Antlers can be used to help communicate, sending and receiving messages from your higher self, your guides, angels, the animal kingdom, and Mother Earth.

FINDING AND USING FEATHERS

Feathers have multiple uses. They can be placed on the altar in the position of the east and the element of air. The element of air is associated with communication and we once used them as quills to pen our own communications. Feathers can be used for contacting other realms as well as Spirit. They can facilitate better communication between two people or a group.

Birds are known to be messengers of Spirit. Feathers can also be a way for a particular bird to send you a message. If you can identify which bird it came from, you can then look up the energies of it to see whether it resonates with you. Sometimes simply holding the feather will allow the message to come through.

Because feathers allow most birds to fly, they can be used to assist with journey work and astral travel. Keeping one in your car can be used to keep you safe while you travel. Blessing one and keeping it by your bed can see you safely in and out of your dreams, including lucid dreaming.

Using found animal items can really add a boost to your magical practice. Use them with the respect that they deserve.

USING ANIMAL IMAGES AND FIGURINES

Another way to bring animal magic into your everyday routine is by keeping images or figurines of animals in your home or at work to add some of their magic to your life. Seeing the image of the wolf every day reminds you to raise your voice and be heard when necessary. It also serves as a symbol of family and their importance in your life. Having a photo of a dove at your work desk can help with peace and harmony. A bear figurine in a child's room can serve as a symbol of a mother bear's protection. Get a keychain with a horse on it for safety while traveling in your vehicle.

GIVING BACK

When you begin to work with the animal kingdom magically,
you will quickly learn that they are eager to help us. When we
call upon them, and even when they simply appear to lend us aid,
it is important that we acknowledge their assistance. A simple
"Thank you" is appreciated as well as offerings. A more impactful
way to show your gratitude to the animal kingdom is by helping
with conservation work. Donating time or money to a reputable
organization or cause is appropriate.

Epilogue

It can be easy to dismiss animals as merely our pets and companions or simply relegate them to their places in the forests, jungles, lakes, and oceans. They are so much more. Science shows us that the animals were here long before we were. They possess wisdom and knowledge that is so ancient it can be difficult for us to fathom. They are a direct link to Mother Earth and the vast information that is stored in her rocks, plants, trees, and the ground beneath our feet.

The animals come to us to assist in delivering messages and sharing this ancient knowledge with us. They can teach us to look at the world and magic in different ways. Animals show us what is right in front of us that we may be missing and they also show us what is beyond what we may be able to see with our own eyes or even our magical and spiritual eyes. They teach us about ourselves and others and show us how to interact with one another and the world around us.

Animals remind us that we all have a little wild in us and that is how it should be. They teach us how to access that wilder side. Witches need to be able to tap into elements and the natural magic that surrounds us. The animals show us the way when we cannot see it ourselves. With their connections to the elements as well as the stars and planets, their magic is boundless.

They can dive into shadow work with us, assist with journeys into other realms to discover new types of energy and magic and how to use it, and travel into our dreams to show us how to process what is going on around us as well as within us. When we align ourselves with the animals, and the energy and magic they bring to us, our own magic can grow in ways we never thought possible.

Magical Knowledge and Reference

Here you will find information on magical days of the week, moon and sun phases/timing, candle magic and corresponding colors, basic herbs, and crystals. All of these can be used alongside animal power to strengthen spells as well as bring your magical workings to the next level. For example, if you are working a protection spell using a black candle dressed with sage and rosemary and perform it on a Saturday, the magic tied to it is some of the most powerful available. If you want to try a communication spell with your animal guide, work it on a Wednesday using a blue candle.

DAYS OF THE WEEK

Each day of the week holds a specific energy. When we align our magical workings to the day that corresponds with what we are trying to achieve, it reinforces the intentions of the spell as well as adding power.

Sunday/The Sun's Day: Divine masculine, success, happiness, joy, vitality, creativity, confidence

Monday/The Moon's Day: Dreams, the subconscious, intuition, scrying, divination, water magic, emotions, women's magic, domestic issues

Tuesday/Mars's Day: When quick action is needed, ambition, sexual potency, passion, personal strength, self-assertion, victory, protection

Wednesday/Mercury's Day: Communication, technology, focus and alertness, learning, writing

Thursday/Jupiter's Day: Luck, abundance and prosperity, increasing and preservation of wealth, business

Friday/Venus's Day: Divine feminine, love, relationships and friendships, beauty, glamor magic, peace, harmony

Saturday/Saturn's Day: Protection, banishing and binding, communing with ancestors and departed spirits, overcoming obstacles

 ## MOON PHASES

As witches, we are well aware of the powerful energies that the moon holds. When we align our spells with the different moon phases, it will further empower them with the energy of that phase. Because many animals have energy that naturally syncs with the moon, they can easily facilitate a deeper working for you.

New or Dark Moon: Setting intentions, manifesting, new beginnings, shadow work

Waxing Crescent: Nurturing, self-love, compassion, courage, positive mindset

First Quarter: Drawing things to you such as a new job, love interest, success, money

Waxing Gibbous: Fertility, endurance, breaking through what one may be resisting

Full Moon: Release, letting go of what no longer serves us, cleansing, protection

Waning Gibbous: Minor banishings, cleansing

Last Quarter: Removing obstacles, allow flow with ease, breaking addictions

Waning Crescent: Major banishings, removing toxic relationships or situations

SUN TIMING

The sun also holds its own powerful energies and we can use specific timing throughout the day to aid our spell and ritual work. You can also connect with solar animal energies, such as the lion, hawk, eagle, scorpion, and ram, to help facilitate sun magic into your workings.

Sunrise/Dawn: New beginnings, manifestation, hope, charging energies

Morning: Growth, building, relationships, wealth

Noon: Protection, justice, health, courage, success

Afternoon: Clarity, resolution, business communication

Sunset: Endings, release, letting go, banishment, divination

CANDLE MAGIC

Candles are commonplace materials when it comes to rituals and spell work. We use them on our altars, to create sacred space, to cast circles, and more. Using various candle colors for a working can be an extremely effective way to boost the spell's power. Like most other things in witchcraft, candles hold their own vibrational patterns and the different colors align with specific magical workings. Use the following candle correspondences for your magical workings.

White: Can be used in place of any other color, healing, spirituality, peace, purity

Black: Protection, banishing, binding, repels negative energies

Brown: Earth energy (grounding), animals and pets, stability, home protection, family

Red: Vitality, passion, romantic love, strength, fast action, courage, root chakra

Pink: Self-love, friendship, emotional healing, nurturing

Yellow: Happiness, joy, success, power, sun energy, solar plexus chakra

Orange: Creativity, self-expression, adventure, positivity, sacral chakra

Green: Nature, physical healing, money (abundance and prosperity), growth, heart chakra

Blue: Communication, inspiration, calming, throat (royal blue) and third eye (indigo) chakras

Purple: Psychic abilities, hidden knowledge, divination, astral projection, crown chakra

Silver: Divine feminine, intuition, dreams, moon energies

Gold: Divine masculine, wealth, luck, happiness, sun energies

DRESSING A CANDLE

Dressing a candle includes the use of an oil and herbs. Typically a carrier oil is used (an oil that is paired with essential oils to dilute them, such as jojoba, sweet almond, or even olive oil) to anoint the candle. This is simply rubbing the candle with the oil and giving it its purpose through stating the intentions of the working. The anointed candle is then rolled in dried herbs that correspond to the spell.

All plants have unique vibrational patterns and properties. Many of them have strong magical energies as well as medicinal uses. The list of magical plants is almost endless, so we'll just cover some of the basics here.

Healing: Angelica, yarrow, echinacea, lemon balm, tansy, rosemary, horehound

Protection: Sage, rosemary, pine, juniper, cedar, garlic, rue, nettles, angelica

Communication: Clary sage, rosemary, bay leaf

Love: Rose (red for romantic or pink for self and friends), lavender, vanilla, basil, jasmine

Money: Basil, cinnamon, bay leaf, mint, juniper, cinquefoil, alfalfa

Divination: Mugwort, rosemary, clary sage, dandelion, star anise

Calming/Sleep: Lavender, chamomile, lemon balm, bergamot, St. John's wort

Fertility: Pine and spruce (to balance masculine and feminine), cinnamon, nettle, vanilla, willow, red and orange rose petals (to activate root and sacral chakras/sex organs)

Happiness: Marjoram, lavender, St. John's wort, mint, lemon balm, pine

Divine Feminine: Spruce, willow, motherwort, jasmine, mugwort, apple

Divine Masculine: Pine, sunflower, mint, bay leaf, basil, St. John's wort, oak leaf

CRYSTAL CORRESPONDENCES

Crystals are powerful magical allies. They protect, help heal, and facilitate communication between our higher self, the Universe, Spirit, and our guides. Combining their energy with other magical tools such as herbs or candle magic and the energy that an animal can lend to you will further empower your workings.

Healing: Amethyst, clear quartz, bloodstone, lepidolite, labradorite, agate, sugilite

Protection: Black obsidian, black tourmaline, smoky quartz, labradorite, jet

Communication: Sodalite, petalite, fluorite, blue lace agate

Love: Rose quartz, garnet, ruby, rhodochrosite, rhodonite

Money: Jade, pyrite, goldstone, emerald, citrine, tiger's eye

Divination: Selenite, moonstone, labradorite, petalite, lapis lazuli

Calming/Sleep: Amethyst, selenite, moonstone, aquamarine, bloodstone

Fertility: Pink tourmaline, red/orange carnelian, moonstone, garnet, green aventurine

Happiness: Citrine, sunstone, dalmatian jasper, tiger's eye

BIBLIOGRAPHY AND REFERENCES

BBC Wildlife Magazine. "Which Animal Sleeps the Most?"
www.discoverwildlife.com/animal-facts/mammals/which-
animal-sleeps-the-most/

Bear, S. L. "Animal Magic: 12 Animals That Can Strengthen Your
Craft." https://thetravelingwitch.com/blog/animal-magic-12-
animals-that-can-strengthen-your-craft

Chavez-Bush, L. "Monkey Buffet Festival." www.atlasobscura.com/
foods/monkey-buffet-festival

Collins, J. "The Power of Totem Animals." www.dw.com/en/global-
ideas-ancient-totem-indian-tribes/a-18364517

"Domestication." Natural Geographic Society. https://education.
nationalgeographic.org/resource/domestication

Driscoll, C. A., J. Clutton-Brock, A. C. Kitchener, and S. J. O'Brien.
"The Evolution of House Cats." *Scientific American*, June 1,
2009. www.scientificamerican.com/article/the-taming-of-
the-cat/

"The Druids." www.classichistory.net/archives/druids

Farquhar, B. "Wolf Reintroduction Changes Ecosystem in
Yellowstone." https://www.yellowstonepark.com/things-to-do/
wildlife/wolf-reintroduction-changes-ecosystem/

Gokun Silver, M. "Once a Year, Thousands of Sheep Take Over
Madrid." *National Geographic-Travel*, September 19, 2017.

"Guisachan Gathering (Golden Retriever Festival)." https://rove.
me/to/scotland/guisachan-gathering

Gurnani, S. "A Guide to Witness the Celebration of Life Itself."
https://traveltriangle.com/blog/velas-turtle-festival/

Hutson, P. "Working with Your Shadow Animal."
https://discover.hubpages.com/religion-philosophy/Working-
With-Your-Shadow-Animal

Kayne, R. "What Is Native American Animal Medicine?"
   https://www.languagehumanities.org/what-is-native-
   american-animal-medicine.htm

Kiehlbauch, S. "Syncretic Animal Symbolism in Medieval
   European Magic." https://core.ac.uk/download/
   pdf/219380849.pdf

Kukharenko, S. P. "Animal Magic: Contemporary Beliefs and
   Practices in Ukrainian Villages." https://journals.ku.edu/
   folklorica/article/view/3784

Kunz, J. "International Animal Festivals." www.lfurl.org/animal-
   festivals-around-world/

Leatsch, D. R. "Origin and History of the Chicken." University of
   Wisconsin-Madison, livestock.extension.wisc.edu

Murphy, K., and Susalla, C. "Secrets of Animal Magic: The
   Power of Spells, Curses, and Omens." https://www.bbc.com/
   historyofthebbc/anniversaries/april/animal-magic/

"National Pig Day." https://nationaltoday.com/national-pig-day/

Schmandt-Besserat, D. "Neolithic Symbolism at Ain Ghazal."
   https://sites.utexas.edu/dsb/ain-ghazal/neolithic-symbolism-
   at-ain-ghazal/

Vanacore, C. B. "Origin and History of Dogs." www.britannica.
   com/animal/dog

Waheed, H., et al. "Snake Venom: From Deadly Toxins to Life-
   saving Therapeutics." National Library of Medicine, https://
   pubmed.ncbi.nlm.nih.gov/28578650, 2017

Williams, S. C. P. "Whence the Domestic Horse?" www.science.
   org/content/article/whence-domestic-horse, May 7, 2012

"Woolly Worm Festival." http://www.woollyworm.com/

"Zoolingualism." https://powerlisting.fandom.com/wiki/
   Zoolingualism

ACKNOWLEDGMENTS

Thank you to my best friend, Coley, my twin flame and the sister of my soul. Thank you for giving me the courage to live life as my authentic self. I appreciate your endless support and love and the knowing that you will always be there for me. Thank you for sharing all the laughs, tears, and adventures on and off the trail. Love you!

To my longtime friend and soul sister, Angie, thank you for those times so long ago when you believed in me and stood by me when no one else did. I wouldn't be where I am today if not for you. I'm so grateful to have you in my life. Love ya!

A personal thank you to my coven, the Silver Phoenixes, that is always there with love and support. Lady Lumosulo, Lady Eala, Lady Rowena Hawkfeather, and Caci: I love and appreciate you all so very much.

I am grateful for the Goddess-given gift of being able to communicate with the animals. I'm thankful for all the messengers and my animal guides and protectors.

Thank you to Quarto Publishing for the opportunity to share this knowledge with you. Thank you to the editors and the design teams that put so much hard work into this book.

INDEX

ABOUT THE AUTHOR

Rieka Moonsong is a Wiccan high priestess and mesa-carrying, Andean-trained shaman. She has made it her life's work to assist others in healing, transforming, and better understanding their true purpose. She offers one-on-one consultations that bring balance and clarity in times of indecision or confusion. Her services include divination, healing, soul work, and more. Her popular Instagram account is @justamountainwitch. She is also the author of *Cat Magick: Harness the Powers of Felines through History, Behaviors, and Familiars.*